GOOD FOOD FROM AUSTRALIA

Hippocrene is NUMBER ONE in

International Cookbooks

Africa and Oceania
Best of Regional African
Cooking
Good Food from Australia
Traditional South African
Cookery

Asia and Near East
Best of Goan Cooking
The Joy of Chinese Cooking
The Art of South Indian
Cooking
The Art of Persian Cooking
The Art of Israeli Cooking
The Art of Turkish Cooking

Mediterranean
Best of Greek Cuisine
Taste of Malta
A Spanish Family Cookbook

Western Europe
Art of Dutch Cooking
Best of Austrian Cuisine
A Belgian Cookbook
Celtic Cookbook
Traditional Recipes from Old
England
The Art of Irish Cooking
Traditional Food from Scotland
Traditional Food from Wales

Scandinavia
Best of Scandinavian Cooking
The Best of Finnish Cooking
The Best of Smorgasbord
Cooking
Good Food from Sweden

Central Europe
All Along the Danube
Bavarian Cooking
Bulgarian Cookbook
The Best of Czech Cooking
The Art of Hungarian Cooking
Polish Heritage Cookery
The Best of Polish Cooking
Old Warsaw Cookbook
Old Polish Traditions
Taste of Romania

Eastern Europe
The Cuisine of Armenia
The Best of Russian Cooking
The Best of Ukrainian Cuisine

Americas
Mayan Cooking
The Honey Cookbook
The Art of Brazilian Cookery
The Art of South American
Cookery

GOOD FOOD
FROM AUSTRALIA

Graeme Newman
and
Betsy Newman

HIPPOCRENE BOOKS
New York

For information, address:
HIPPOCRENE BOOKS, INC.
171 Madison Avenue
New York, NY 10016

Library of Congress Cataloging-in-Publication Data
Newman, Graeme and Newman, Betsy
    Good food from Australia: a down under cookbook / Graeme
Newman and Betsy Newman. —Hippocrene pbk. ed.
    p. cm.
    Rev. ed. of: The down under cookbook / Graeme Newman. c 1987.
    Includes index.
    ISBN 0-7818-0491-4
    1. Cookery, Australian. 2. Australia—Social life and customs.
I. Newman, Graeme R. II. Newman, Graeme, R. Down under cookbook.
III. Title.
TX725.A9N44   1996
641.5994—dc20   96-21464

Printed in the United States of America.

Acknowledgments

The authors are grateful to Keith McKenry and Bunyip Bush Enterprises for permission to reproduce "At the Sign of the Ravenous Goanna," taken from *The Spirit of the People: Modern Australian Recitations*, 1983.

Contents

*Dedicated to the mums of history
who gave their lives
to the kitchen*

At The Sign of the Ravenous Goanna

At the sign of the Ravenous Goanna
I went to have a feed:
The thought was so exquisite
I was trembling at the knees.

They have Lamingtons in Batter,
And Licorice All-sorts Pie,
And Lamb's Fry served in Cold Custard
That you just have to try.

Vegemite, and Lipton's Tea
Dished up with Rabbit Stew,
And Two Fruits, lovely Two Fruits,
To thrill you through and through.

Tomato Sauce and Chocolate Frogs,
And Saunder's Malt Extract
(Just pity all the poor lost souls
Who've never tasted that!)

Dims Sims, Chooks, and Chico Rolls,
And good old boiled Galah;
Floaters and Vick's Vapo-Rub
For old men with catarrh.

Polly Waffles, Prickly Pear,
Johnny Cakes and Billy Tea;

GOOD FOOD FROM AUSTRALIA

Stewed Prune and Baked Bean Jaffles
—Oh, Australian food for me!

There's Scotty's Wild Stuff Stew of course,
And Oysters from the Rocks,
And Wine, the nectar of the Grape,
Served from a cardboard box.

Peck's Fish Paste and Passion Fruit;
Teddy Bears with Robur Tea;
Pavlova, Chips and Choo-Choo Bars
—The Height of Luxury!

Yabbies, Jaffas, Saveloys,
Damper, Crays, Nardoo;
Jumbuk Pate for the pseudes,
Butter Menthols for the 'flu.

There's a dish for every taste and mood,
And they sing Australian songs.
So come to the Ravenous Goanna, friends,
And bring your friends along.
—*Keith McKenry, 1970s*

Chapter 1

The Aussie Way

*T*he winds of a million years have made Australia into what she is today. There are few jagged peaks in the outback. Instead, there are rocky outcrops worn round and smooth by the endless grinding of the elements. The reds of the Australian center are matched in tone and intensity only by the scorched surface of Mars. It is a timeless land, as the great Australian novelist Eleanor Dark observed many years ago.

The Australian Aborigines are Australia's timeless people, the original Australians. There are many aboriginal folk stories that preserve a sense of the sheer age of the land and her people, often referred to as the "dream time"(see Dream Cake, page 183). Australia's unusual animals loom large in these stories, and well they should.

Australia boasts animal species that are unique: furred animals that lay eggs (the platypus); others that suckle their young in pouches (kangaroos); still others that get high on a naturally found drug (koalas); birds whose calls sound as raucous laughter (kookaburra); yet other birds that mimic all the sounds of the bush (the lyre bird).

Into this giant landscape stepped the English, in the 1770s, searching for somewhere to dump their convicts. The American Revolution made it impossible for the English to use America as its prison. There are many theories as to how the Australian national character—carefree (epitomized by the common saying, "She'll be right mate"), a bit abrasive and a most disarming, earthy, sense of humor—has evolved from that of criminals. Sir Robert Menzies (Australia's conservative prime minister for some 18 years ending in 1966) was always ready with an answer to those who made fun of Australia's convict ancestry. In a speech at the Jefferson Oration at Charlottesville, Virginia on the 4th of July, 1963, Sir Robert wryly noted, "... the records show that the great majority of persons convicted in England during the transportation era remained in England...."

The influence of the English on Australian lifestyles and customs is vast. We have them to thank for the national sport of cricket. Australia's unique sport, "Aussie Rules" football was derived from Irish football. And we have the English to thank for our Irish heritage, since a large portion of convicts sent to Australia were Irish. Our rich array of folk songs and poetry are directly attributable to the oppression of convicts and settlers by the British and their lackeys in the early colonial period.

Most of all, though, the English have influenced Australian food, cooking, and eating habits. Many of the oldest recipes in this book bear a strong similarity to English dishes. Fruit cake, steamed pudding, roast lamb, pasties, and many others, are directly identifiable in English cuisine. But they have also become a central feature in traditional Australian cuisine, and are reasonably included as "Australian."

Traditional Australian Cooking

What is an authentic Australian dish? The answer to this difficult question is, any dish that Australians have taken to call their own. A dish that they eat as part of everyday life. Fish and Chips are English. But they are Australian, too, and Australians have given them their special Australian "character," if one can refer to a French fry as having character. (Does one ever hear the claim that the English chip is really French?)

Older recipes form the major part of this book because it is our aim to preserve the traditional Australian way of cooking that we think is probably fast disappearing, supplanted by exotic dishes from the far East and Europe. In the broad balance of things, this change is, of course a good thing, because the range of dishes available to the Australian cook and diner is now just wonderful. Australian cities boast some of the best restaurants in the world. One can walk down any street in Australia's major cities (indeed, in country towns) and find restaurants from many different cultures from around the world. This is why we have included a separate chapter in this new edition of the cookbook, to reflect these recent changes. We have also expanded the "Outback Cooking" chapter to include "modern Australian" recipes, those that attempt to rediscover the indigenous Australian foods.

The traditional recipes in this book were gleaned from personal recipe files of friends and relatives. Sometimes these recipes have been a bit hard to decipher. Our parents and grandparents cooked most of their lives on a wood burning stove and oven. Their handwritten recipes mostly said, "warm," "moderate,"or "hot" oven—not very precise. The way they established whether the oven was ready, was to open the door and put in their hand. It has been a bit of a challenge to translate these imprecise meas-urements into temperature settings.

The quantities are also difficult to translate because old Aus-tralian measurements (modern Australian is now completely metric), especially tablespoons, dessertspoons, and liquid meas-ures are quite different from those found in America. We have tried to convert these measures accurately, but just in case we have messed up here or there, we suggest that you treat the measurements of the older traditional recipes as guides to be adjusted if you think things are not going quite right.

The Australian Outback and Bush Cooking

Eighty percent of Australia's population of 18 million live in its five largest cities. This makes Australia one of the most sparsely populated, yet most urbanized, countries in the world!

Many Australians have probably never seen a kangaroo in the wild (though if you know where to go, this is quite a simple thing to do), and would never even think of trying to live in the outback. There are not really many _authentic_ outback recipes, though there has been a recent renaissance in genuine Australian cooking. Some popular restaurant chains, one even in America, now boast Australian menus. These are modern, rather than traditional recipes. Most use a few traditional outback ingredients (such as witchetty grubs) and produce a modern dish which largely masks the taste of the original ingredient. Many of the authentic outback dishes can be cooked in America, although a few of the ingredients aren't available in the American forest, such as tiger snake. Substitutions can be made, though. If you really must have it, it is now possible to order and import such delicacies as witchetty grubs from Australia. We have included a number of these "new traditional"recipes in Chapter 13.

The Australian Language ("Strine") and Cooking Traditions

Americans frequently ask whether Australians speak English. The answer is, "More or less." Of course, we do speak English, but with a heavy accent, with the voice directed somewhere down one's chest. If you say "newspiper" instead of "newspaper"you will have closely reproduced the typical Australian vowel sound. However, it is not so much the accents that make Australians difficult to understand, but the many unique expressions. There is a whole vocabulary, along with unusual usage of common words that can make conversation with an Australian something of an experience. An American friend once gave a speech to a large audience of Australian police, urging that people get off their fannies and work for a particular project. He was unaware that "fanny"does not mean "backside" in Australia as it does in the U.S., but rather refers to a very private female part!

Throughout the book we have included notations on Australian language, without which it would be difficult to describe eating and cooking traditions. Accordingly, we could say, "bon appetit" but the Australian saying is more earthy, in keeping with our convict ancestry:

Two, Four, Six, Eight,
Bog in, don't wait!

... and enjoy your tucker (food)!

Platypus

Chapter 2

Pie 'n Sauce...and Other Aussie Classics

*T*o be "fair dinkum" in the ustralian language is to be "true blue." None the wiser? Both expressions mean absolutely pure and authentic. And that's what these foods are. They're pure Australian. It doesn't matter that they may have existed somewhere else (in once-Great Britain, for example) long before they became part of every Australian's life. What is important is that they *are now* totally unique to Australia. A spectator sport would be unthinkable without them—just as a baseball game would be unthinkable without hot dogs.

Should you go to the cricket or footy (an Australian Rules football game) you will have many chances to buy a pie and sauce (and, if you're that way inclined, a can of Fosters beer to go with it). Meat pies are the take-out food in Australia. Some tasteless people, certainly not dinkum Aussies, have described Aussie meat pies as gravy encased in pieces of cardboard pastry. This may (only *may*) be true for mass-produced pies, but it certainly is not true for those made at home.

MAISIE'S PASTIES

Pronounced *pah-stees*, these are probably of Cornish origin, but are definitely now Australian through and through. They are sometimes a different shape than that described in this recipe, which is the typical Cornish pasty shape.

Along with fish and chips, and hot dogs and pies, pasties are a favorite take-out food in Australia. Their aroma while cooking is nothing short of tantalizing. The unusual blend of vegetables and meat, encased in a delicious pastry makes them unique as take-out food—and probably the most nutritious. These days, vegetarian pasties are quite common.

Of all childhood memories, those involving taste stand out, and for Aussies, those of sniffing pasties while cooking are by far and away the most prominent. It took a long time to get this recipe into some form that was dependable, as Maisie did not use exact measurements. One simply sifted some flour and margarine, mixed up the vegetables, and there it was. The oven temperature was also difficult to establish, because old-time cooks used the hand in the wood-burning oven as the oven thermometer.

One of us has found, with much disappointment, that some Americans do not like pasties, and even Australians raised in the United States are not too thrilled about them. This seems to be because of the turnip or rutabaga, which are not common vegetables. One could make them without these vegetables, but then the pasties would lose their distinctive taste. Pasties are eaten with plenty of ketchup (*tomato sauce* to Australians). Some like them made with lots of pepper.

Filling:
1 carrot
1 small turnip or rutabaga
2 to 3 onions
1 pound potatoes
1 pound lean ground beef
salt and pepper

- Chop finely or mince all vegetables and add to meat. Mix thoroughly, add salt and pepper.

Pastry:
2 cups self-rising flour
1 pinch salt
½ pound (two sticks) margarine
1/3 cup water
Egg or milk for brushing tops

- Sift flour and salt, rub in margarine until mixture looks like bread crumbs. Mix in water gradually, stirring with a wooden spoon until dough makes a stiff ball. If in doubt, it is better that the dough is a little moist than dry. Turn onto floured board and knead lightly. Cut into 12 pieces and knead into rounds. Roll out each round as thin as possible but be sure that the dough can be lifted and shaped without breaking. Spoon filling into center of each piece of dough, then with wet finger, moisten the edges of each dough round. Lift pastry up from sides, bringing into the center, and pinch together all across the top. Begin at center and work towards the outside. Instead of pinching together at the top, sometimes the mixture is placed on one side of the round, and the other half folded all the way over and pinched around the edge, making a kind of half circle shape (something like an apple turnover). Puff pastry is also sometimes used. Place pasties on greased cookie tray. Paint with egg or milk, then prick tops with fork. Bake for 30 to 45 minutes at 350 to 400 degrees, until pastry is golden brown.

Makes 12 pasties.

PIE AND SAUCE

Here is an all-time favorite recipe. It is for a 9-inch pie pan. The pies one may buy in the store are usually a small one-serving size. The traditional shape is oval, but this tradition disappeared many years ago, no doubt because the shape could not be adapted easily to mass production. Bought pies also have a pie crust on top and bottom, otherwise they would be difficult to eat in the hands. Even so, they are really hard to bite into without gravy shooting out over your shirt.

½ to ¾ pounds ground beef or cubed steak
1 tablespoon flour
1 tablespoon butter
2 tablespoons finely chopped onion
¼ cup finely chopped celery
¼ cup finely chopped carrots
1 cup beef stock
salt and pepper
1 recipe pastry (see Maisie's Pasties, page 20)

- Roll beef in flour, or sprinkle 1 tablespoon of flour over ground beef. Sauté beef in butter with onion, celery and carrot, until meat is brown and vegetables are bright in color. Cover with beef stock, add salt and pepper to taste, and simmer, covered, until meat is tender. Place in greased pie pan and top with pie crust. Bake for 10 to 15 minutes at 425 degrees or until pastry is golden brown. Serve hot, always with plenty of ketchup (*tomato sauce* in Australia).

Makes one 9-inch pie.

For STEAK AND KIDNEY PIE, the English ancestor of these pies, add 1 small chopped beef kidney to meat mixture.

Many variations are possible with this recipe. If you are entertaining, line muffin tins with thin pastry, fill with pie filling, and cap. These party pies are always a raving success. Try other variations: add a couple of spoonfuls of frozen peas to the mixture 5 minutes before meat is cooked. Better still, when sautéing meat and vegetables, add 1 tablespoon of red wine, preferably claret. Or, try a teaspoon of port (yes, port). Can be frozen and reheated a week or two later.

MOM'S SAUSAGE ROLLS

We have eaten these little beauties in New Zealand, Scotland, England, Canada, and even in Delaware, USA. While always delicious, the commercial variety never tastes the same as the real Australian, homemade sausage roll, especially the ones Mom used to make. The difference is in the pastry.

1 recipe pastry (see Maisie's Pasties, page xx)
½ pound sausage meat
1 tablespoon flour
1 egg yolk

- Roll out pastry into oblong shape and cut into 8 even pieces by cutting first straight down the center of pastry, then across 3 times. Divide sausage meat into 8 pieces, roll each piece into a sausage shape and sprinkle all over with flour. Place each sausage on pastry, moisten edges of pastry with water. Fold over pastry so that it covers sausage and meets on other side (see illustration). Press together with back of a flat knife. Beat egg yolk and brush on rolls. Bake in 375- to 400-degree oven for 20 to 30 minutes.

Makes 8 rolls.

SECRET: Make sure your pastry is not too short (too dry), or it will be difficult to work over sausage, and will also crumble when your eager guests try to get their mouths around these delicious morsels. There may also be a problem with the sausage meat. In Australia this meat is usually finely ground beef, but sometimes pork is used. We have tried pork sausage in the United States, which is fine, but be sure you buy extra lean, otherwise you may end up with sausage rolls floating around in a sea of fat. Ideally, the sausage should be finely ground as in pork sausage, but shaped lean ground beef, while not perfect, still provides a delicious roll. Link sausages are also O.K.

When you are accomplished at rolling the dough very thin, little party sausage rolls are a popular item. They are also wonderful cold—perfect for a midnight snack. Sausage rolls are always eaten with plenty of ketchup.

Pasty   Sausage Roll

PORK PIES

4 ounces pork
½ apple
½ onion
2 tablespoons flour
salt and pepper
½ cup water
1 recipe pastry (see Maisie's Pasties, page 20)
milk for top

- Mince the pork, or ask your butcher to do it for you. Chop apple and onion very fine, add flour, salt and pepper, and water, mixing well. Simmer until apple and onion are soft. Line 1 well-greased muffin pan with thin pie crust. Fill with mixture and cover with pastry. Paint tops with milk, and prick with fork. Bake in oven at 375 to 400 degrees for an hour.

Makes 6 small pies.

ABOUT PORK PIES: Pork pies are definitely not a part of Australian cooking any more. They are certainly still very much a part of the English scene. One can find them along with Scotch eggs in just about every English pub. Not so in Australia. Old Australians consider pork to be very "sickly"— only to be eaten on very special occasions. In fact, Australian pork does tend to be less lean than its American counterpart. But, in deference to our wonderful English heritage, we include this recipe for pork pies. Actually, they're delicious. They probably were edged out of Australian pubs by beef pies and pasties which do go better with beer. Pork pies taste better with apple cider (effervescent and alcoholic, of course).

EGG AND BACON PIE

The chances are that, just as in the United States, real Australian men don't eat quiche. But you can be sure that they *do* eat egg and bacon pie which is very similar, if not better than quiche. Try it, and decide for yourself.

1 recipe pastry (see Maisie's Pasties, page 20)
4 large eggs
¼ cup grated cheddar cheese
1 small onion, finely chopped
½ cup milk
salt and pepper
2 tablespoons chopped parsley
½ cup chopped bacon (lean is best)

- Roll out pastry thin and line a 9-inch pie pan. Place eggs, cheese, onions, milk, and salt and pepper in pan and beat with a fork until blended well. Heat over low flame, like you would cook scrambled eggs. Stir continually. When mixture has consistency of lightly scrambled eggs, mix in parsley. Pour into pie pan and cover with pieces of bacon. Bake at 350 degrees for 30 minutes. It's O.K. to eat this pie with ketchup. This is a wonderful dish to cook for house guests who don't usually eat breakfast. The aroma will reach everyone's bedroom and to their surprise they will find themselves irresistibly drawn to the brekkie (breakfast) table.

VARIATION: After pouring egg mixture into pie shell, break 4 eggs onto the top of the mixture. Cook as above.
Makes one 9-inch pie.

RUPANYUP RISSOLES

These are interesting hybrids, half hamburger and half croquette. Traditional Aussie moms used to make rissoles often, using minced up or diced leftover meat, whether lamb, veal, or beef. In fact, this was the original ingredient for rissoles, just as leftover meat was traditionally used for that other favorite, Shepherd's Pie. We haven't included the latter in this book, because just about every American cookbook one opens has a recipe for it. The brown gravy (called *Gravox)* can also be bought in powder form in Australian shops. It makes a delicious gravy with a more homestyle flavor than gravy mixes found in American stores.

Meat patties:
¼ pound ground beef
½ teaspoon basil
up to one cup torn bread
2 tablespoons finely chopped parsley
1 egg
bread crumbs
1/3 cup beef bouillon

- Lightly brown ground beef over high heat. Add basil, bread, parsley, and egg, lower heat and stir until mixture is quite thick, like cold, cooked oatmeal. Add bread crumbs or bouillon until correct thickness is obtained. Remove from pan and set aside to cool.

For dipping:
4 tablespoons flour
salt and pepper
1 egg
½ cup bread crumbs
2 tablespoons parsley

- Take large tablespoons of the meat mixture, form into patties, and roll in the flour, salt, and pepper. Beat egg and brush over rissole, then roll in bread crumbs, pushing crumbs onto surface with a knife. Heat cooking oil, and when quite hot place rissoles in pan and fry each side until golden brown. When cooked, drain on paper, serve garnished with parsley, and with brown sauce (below). Ketchup or a packet of brown gravy is also fine.

Makes 4 to 5 rissoles.

BROWN SAUCE

¼ cup carrot
¼ cup rutabaga
¼ cup onion
¼ cup celery
1 tablespoon chopped parsley
1 teaspoon thyme
¼ teaspoon marjoram
2 bay leaves
4 peppercorns
1 tablespoon oil
1 small tomato
2 tablespoons flour
salt and pepper
1 ¼ cups beef bouillon
1 slice bacon

- Chop vegetables. Tie up herbs in small cloth bag. Dry vegetables with paper towel. Heat oil and fry all vegetables, except tomato, until a light brown. Stir frequently. Add tomato and stir a little more. Add flour, salt and pepper, to taste, and brown well. Pour in bouillon, stirring until it boils. Add herbs and bacon, then simmer for 30 minutes. Strain and remove fat. Serve separately, or pour over rissoles. Minced or chopped leftover meat may be substituted for the ground beef.

ABOUT RUPANYUP: These rissoles are named in honor of Rupanyup, a small town in the Wimmera district of Victoria, one of Australia's smallest states (only Tasmania is smaller). This is the heart of the wheat-growing district, a country of wide, flat plains, golden with wheat, and rich red earth. Cockatoos flock in great white clouds, shrieking loudly to show off their dominance in this great landscape.

TOAD IN THE HOLE

This meat and batter dish is popular for breakfast, lunch, or dinner.

½ cup self-rising flour
2 tablespoons margarine, melted
¾ cup milk (warm)
1 egg, beaten
salt
½ pound sausage meat

- Sift flour, add the margarine, and gradually add milk. Beat well, fold in egg just before using, and add salt to taste. Shape sausage meat into sausage shapes. Grease baking pan and place in a 400-degree oven until very hot. Pour in the batter, drop in the sausages so that they lie in one direction. Bake for 35 minutes. Best served with thick brown gravy, or ketchup.

Makes 4 servings.

ABOUT SAUSAGE MEAT: You will have to experiment with sausage meat. If you decide to use pork sausage, ask your butcher for pork sausage that is very lean, otherwise you may have underground rivers of fat, rather than toads in the hole. If you would rather play it safe, the older, though less common Australian version of this dish-with-the-strange-name is made with pieces of good quality steak or cubed lamb. We use extra-lean ground beef.

Yes, this dish is also essentially English in origin. The Australian version is far better, though, because it uses snags (the long thin ones) as the sausage meat. Sausage links could be substituted. Aussie kids of old used to plead with their moms to make this dish. They had fun searching for the "toads."

Chapter 3

Sandwiches and Scones

*A*merican friends who have visited Australia have been shocked at what they rather uncharitably termed "the little things Australians call sandwiches." Not only are they the wrong *size,* they say, but they are often the wrong *color*!

When friends and relatives from Australia visit us here, they are aghast at the amount of filling and in sheer size of American sandwiches. One becomes accustomed to the (roughly), quarter pound of cold cuts in a sandwich served in a typical deli in the American northeast. When they see these sandwiches, Australian visitors spend much of the rest of their visit pointing out all the fat Americans they can, and trying to order half a sandwich. We'd rather not take sides in the serious difference in values between our two countries, but we think we can say why there is such a difference—or at least why the Australian sandwiches are so small.

There are basically two kinds of sandwiches in Australia: those that are cut by thousands of moms every day for school and work lunches, and those prepared for afternoon teas. There is not a great deal of difference between the two, as far as fillings go, but they are both vastly different from an American sandwich. Here's why.

Australian sandwiches are almost always cut from a small-size sandwich loaf (the most common are white and "wholemeal" though these days there is about as big a variety of bread as in America). Without exception, the bread for every sandwich is cut thinner than in America, in fact the thinner the better.

In addition, each slice of bread is spread with a thin layer of butter or margarine. Again, this is without exception, no matter the filling — even peanut butter.

If one is preparing sandwiches for an afternoon tea or a kid's birthday party (yes, believe it or not, there are sandwiches that are quite acceptable to kids for a birthday party—read on!), the practice is to cut off all the crusts, making the overall size of the bread slice even smaller. Then the sandwiches are cut diagonally so that small dainty triangles are produced. Squares and rectangles are also acceptable, but they are the exception.

Now for the "meager fillings." It is largely because of the butter in the sandwiches that there is less filling. If one buys a roast beef sandwich in Australia one may receive two or three slices, four at the most in the sandwich. It is not quantity that is important, but a particular taste. We should add that meats tend to be much more cooked in Australia than the United States. Anyway it is probably the acquired taste of butter in the sandwich that satisfies the Australian appetite. If there were any more filling, the sandwich would be too sickly.

The more usual sandwich lunch would be "two rounds of sandwiches" (although the sandwiches are square, not round). This means 4 slices of bread made into two sandwiches, each sandwich possibly with a different filling, but a filling no more than $\frac{1}{4}$ inch thick. In a sandwich shop, packets of mixed sandwiches are common. Again, these will have very meager fillings, by American standards, but will have three or four different fillings, and will usually contain 2 rounds of sandwiches (i.e., 4 slices of bread).

Sandwiches for Special Occasions

These are always cut into dainty sizes, as described above, and served in the afternoon with a cup of tea, if for an adult occasion. The most famous is the Vegemite Sandwich introduced, at least in name, to curious Americans by the *Men At Work* singing group.

Vegemite Sandwich

It says on the Vegemite jar label that this dark, iodine colored substance is a vegetable yeast extract. Folklore has it that many years ago, a bright young chemist developed it from the enormous amounts of byproducts from beer manufacture. Perhaps you have not heard, but Australians are devoted beer drinkers.

For special occasions, which include parties, special teas, or for someone who is feeling down (Vegemite is the chicken soup of Australian Moms) these sandwiches are often served open style. The bread should be as fresh as possible.

Spread bread lightly with butter or margarine. Place a small amount of Vegemite on the tip of a knife and spread very thinly over bread and butter. Cut into dainty shapes. Butter and Vegemite may also be spread on any type of cracker. Be warned! We have not met many Americans who liked this stuff. It's a taste that is carefully cultivated among Australian kids virtually from birth. It also tastes very salty, although now there is a version that is low salt.

ABOUT VEGEMITE. Vegemite is a trademark of Kraft Foods (believe it or not!). It may be found occasionally in American gourmet food stores, although its (lesser) counterpart, Marmite (a beef extract a bit like bouillon paste) is more common (also English and not Australian, therefore naturally of less importance). To find out all about Vegemite go to the Vegemite web site: http://www.ozchannel.com/vegemite/vegemite.html.

Hundreds and Thousands (Fairy Bread)

Spread fresh slices of both brown and white bread lightly with butter. Top with a generous amount of rainbow sprinkles (called "hundreds and thousands" in Australia), and cut into dainty sizes. Do not try to spread after you have put on the sprinkles, or the colors will run. Chocolate sprinkles are also enjoyed, although the expression "hundreds and thousands" is a term most often associated with very special occasions like kids' birthday parties.

Tomato Sandwiches

Slice bread (the freshest possible—there's nothing worse than tomato sandwiches on day-old bread) as thinly as possible. Spread each slice with butter or margarine. Select a firm ripe tomato and slice very thinly. Place one layer of tomato on bread, sprinkle with salt and pepper to taste, close sandwich, cut into triangles.

No, nothing has been left out. On occasion one of us asks for a grilled tomato sandwich at a local cafeteria, and always get the response, "You mean cheese and tomato?" Sometimes it's easier to ask for a BLT without lettuce, bacon, or mayo but with a little butter! It's an expensive way to buy it, but sometimes it's the only way one can convince the waitress (or the chef) to prepare a sandwich with just tomato! One is, though, mostly disappointed when the sandwich comes. The tomato is always cut too thick. To reproduce the Australian sandwich the tomato must be sliced very thin.

Tomato sandwiches are virtually the staple Australian food (excluding beer, that is). We wouldn't mind ten cents for each one we ate when we went to school. We are of the impression that this tradition may be under slow transition toward mixing other fillings with the tomato, the most popular being ham.

Australian sandwich

Other Sandwich Fillings

Try these fillings in your small, thin sandwiches. Remember to butter the bread. When making these sandwiches at home, Aussies would probably not mix the fillings. These days, at a sandwich shop, one is offered these and many other fillings, and customers commonly request many different combinations of fillings.

diced asparagus (a Queensland favorite in season)
processed cheese and diced celery
tomato and cucumber
cucumber
sardines
Vegemite and cheese
corned beef and pickles
apples and raisins
cheese and raisins
ham and mustard
diced boiled eggs and lettuce
German sausage and ketchup*
cold leftover spaghetti
cold baked beans
salmon
potted steak (see recipe page 38)

American sandwich

German sausage is the Australian equivalent to bologna sausage. The taste is a little more spiced, but the consistency of the sausage is very similar. Ketchup is called *tomato sauce* in Australia.

A few of these fillings may seem a little "yucky" to you, especially the cold spaghetti. Remember, these sandwiches have very little filling, less than ¼ an inch at the most. You'll be surprised how good they taste.

Some of these sandwiches are not so good for school or work lunches. Cucumber and tomato tend to soak through the bread and turn it to slop. These have to be made and eaten quickly.

POTTED STEAK

This is a very, very old recipe that our grandmothers used to make. We doubt that mothers (or fathers) of today either have the time or want to make the time to cook this delicacy of old.

1 pound lean steak
4 tablespoons Worcestershire sauce
½ cup (1 stick)butter
¾ teaspoon cayenne pepper
½ teaspoon mace
½ teaspoon ground nutmeg
salt to taste

- Trim fat off meat, cut into small squares. Add all ingredients and simmer in a deep pot for 4 hours. Mince twice and mix into own gravy. Do not add water. Place in bowl, cover, and refrigerate. When set, may be used as cold meat sliced for salads. Or, may be used as a spread for sandwiches.
Serves 6 to 8.

Old Australian menus did not often include paté, as known in French cuisine. However, the wide variety of potted meats available in Australia more than made up for this gap. An exception is a product called Peck's Paste, a perennial favorite for a couple of generations. These pastes are sold in the supermarket, and there are many varieties, including fish paste, chicken, ham, and other combinations. Their consistency and spiced flavor makes them not unlike their (distant) cousin, French paté. Needless to say, if used for sandwiches, the bread is always buttered, and only a thin spread of these pastes is applied.

AUSSIE-BURGER WITH THE WORKS

Hamburgers are about as American as one can get, though the name of this recipe obviously is not American. Now that a certain fast-food chain has moved into Australia, the (almost) indigenous Australian hamburger is on the road to extinction, if this has not occurred already.

An American friend who went on a business trip to Sydney some years ago would no doubt applaud this Darwinian fate of the Aussieburger. This is because he thinks that they are the wrong color! (We'll explain why shortly).

1 onion, finely chopped
1 small carrot, grated
1 tablespoon vegetable oil
1 pound lean ground beef
1 egg
1 small can beets
lettuce, ketchup, tomato, fried eggs, hard rolls

* Lightly sauté onion and carrot in vegetable oil, allow to cool. In large bowl, thoroughly mix ground beef (called "mince-meat" in Australia), lightly beaten egg, onion, and carrot. Press into patties and broil or fry according to taste.
Makes 4 to 6 burgers.

While this recipe is not especially different from any recipe one would find in an American cookbook, there is one ingredient sneaked into the burger that sets it apart, and ruins its color—beets. In Australia, beet root (as beets are called) rears its ugly, velvety-red head in many unexpected places. When our American friend ordered an Aussieburger and replied that, yes, he would have it with the works, liberal amounts of beet root were inserted along with the salad. Unlike other hamburger ingredients, such as lettuce or tomato, beet root won't keep to itself. It seeps everywhere, and colors most of the hamburger purple! Our American friend announced that he hated beets in sandwiches because they wouldn't mind their own business. Australians not only enjoy beets in their hamburgers, they even eat beet sandwiches!

A final difference between Australian and American hamburgers is that traditional Aussieburgers always used hard rolls, or at least they did in the old days (when they were sold at the late night stands on Saturdays in downtown Melbourne). Now that the fast food-chains have moved in, all this is changing, since the hamburgers at these places, as far as one can tell, are exactly the same as in America. By the way, traditional Aussieburgers are the only sandwiches that Australians don't put butter on. Cheese is also used rarely, and fried eggs have always been popular.

SALAD ROLLS

On the few occasions when kids our age used to buy their lunch at school, we would look forward to a salad roll (for one of us, without beet root, thank you!). These rolls are simple to make, and today, because they have nothing but vegetables in them, might be seen as the food of vegetarians. But they have been around and popular in Australia long before the health food craze came in, and existed side by side the ever popular consumption of meat. As simple as the ingredients seem, these rolls are delicious. Beet root, of course, remains a vital ingredient. Australians just love these rolls with lavish amounts of this all-embracing vegetable. Of course, there is nothing to stop one from adding one's favorite cold cuts. Chicken or ham are a popular addition to this vegetarian fare.

    beets
    fresh crisp lettuce
    thinly sliced firm tomato
    grated carrot
    thinly sliced cucumber
    well-chopped onion
    thin slice of orange
    hard rolls
    Butter

These vegetables and fruits should be placed in hard crisp rolls that have been lavishly spread with butter or margarine. One may have difficulty finding rolls that are similar to those used in Australia. The closest we found are called "crispy torpedoes" at our local Italian bakery. Add salt and pepper to taste. Salad dressing would not normally be added—the butter serves this purpose. Many of the Australian hard crispy rolls are round, not submarine shaped. Except for the shape, one can see that these salad rolls are a close cousin to the popular American submarine sandwich.

GRILLED CHEESE

A grilled cheese sandwich is not the same in Australia as it is in America. This is because the word "grill" has a slightly different meaning. In Australian cooking, to grill food is usually to broil it. A grilled cheese sandwich is mostly done open style, so that the cheese melts into the bread and browns as well.

thick slices of bread
butter
slices of processed cheese

- Place slices of bread under broiler and toast one side only. Remove, spread lightly with butter, cover with one or two (no more!) slices of cheese. Return to broiler and toast until cheese melts or browns on top. Cut into squares, serve immediately. This dish does not keep well. Cook and eat quickly. Popular in Australia for a quick snack or lunch.

ON THE DIFFERENCE BETWEEN GRILLED AND TOASTED SANDWICHES: A grilled sandwich in America is cooked in a hot pan. Each side of the sandwich is lightly buttered, then the sandwich is browned on the hot surface. The number of sandwiches in America that are cooked in this way are limited mainly to variations of grilled cheese, and sometimes with corned beef or ham, and of course the ever popular Reuben. In Australia, sandwiches grilled American style are uncommon.

Australian toasted sandwiches, sometimes called grilled sandwiches (because "grill" often means "broil"), are very popular, especially for tea, if it is the family custom, (as it was ours for many years), to have the main meal at midday and a light meal in the evening.

If the terminology here is confusing, we're not surprised. We have never quite figured it all out. Aussies call their kids in for "tea" which means the evening meal. We once invited American friends to "tea." They arrived at the appointed hour (6:30 P.M.)

having eaten a large dinner. They thought we had invited them for a cup of tea! They had pained looks on their faces when we served up a large, three-course dinner!

We should also distinguish the Australian toasted sandwich from the sandwich that one might order in America, by saying something like, "BLT on whole wheat toast, please." In America, they toast the bread separately, then make the sandwich. In Australia, we make the sandwich, then toast the whole darn thing. All sandwiches may from time to time be treated in this way, but the out-and-out favorites are cheese, tomato, and ham. We have even known some to eat toasted peanut butter sandwiches. Don't forget to butter the bread.

Grilled Cheese

DAD'S SCONES

"Scone" rhymes with "gone" in Australian. It should be the same in America, Americans usually say "scone" more like "cone." "Scone" also has other meanings in Australian. To "do one's scone" is to lose one's temper. One can also have "a thick scone," which means to be thick in the head. As we have noted elsewhere (see Chapter 8 on cookies) that a scone is almost the same as an American biscuit.

Every kid who takes a home economics course in Australia is sure to have learned to make scones. For reasons difficult to understand, they are widely considered the most elementary of cooking skills. But they are very difficult to cook well. There is a lot of folklore about how to make scones turn out light and fluffy. We've tried them all, but more often than one would like, they turn out like—well, rocks. We are not surprised, therefore, when we visit the "upscale" coffee shops, now popular throughout America, that the scones proffered for sale are almost invariably hard as rocks, and difficult to digest. We have also sampled the Aussie "toaster biscuits" found in various supermarkets through-out the U.S. These, of course, have never been heard of by ordinary Aussies. They do, though, retain the distinctive taste of the Aussie scone. But the consistency (and of course the shape) are different.

    1 teaspoon white vinegar
    2 cups milk
    3 cups self rising flour
    6 tablespoons margarine
    melted butter or milk for top

- Mix vinegar with milk to curdle. Sift flour, rub in margarine until mixture is like oatmeal. Add milk gradually and work in with wooden spoon. Work dough until it becomes sloppy and sticks to the fingers. Sprinkle flour on board and knead dough until it is no longer sticky on the outside. Pat out to about 1 inch thick, and cut with a glass dipped in flour or round cookie cutter. Preheat oven to 450 degrees. Lightly grease cookie tray, and place in oven to warm a little. Place scones on tray, arranging so they almost touch. Paint tops with melted butter or milk. Place on top rung of oven, cook 8 to 10 minutes. Dad says that the trick is to make sure your oven is *very* hot. Depending on your oven, you might even need to make it a little hotter than 450 degrees. Do not allow to cool on tray. Immediately remove and place, preferably, in a wicker-type basket, wrapped lightly in a thin cloth. Serve warm if possible.

Makes 12 scones.

Scones

ELSIE'S SCONES

1 cup self-rising flour
1 cup whole wheat flour
1 teaspoon sugar
6 to 8 tablespoons butter
Water as needed

* Sift flours and sugar into a bowl and rub butter into mixture until it has consistency of oatmeal. Slowly, in small amounts, add water, mixing until a soft dough is obtained. Tip out onto board and knead well. Roll out to about 1 inch thick, cut into circles. Preheat oven to 400 degrees. Place on greased cookie tray, bake 10 minutes in hot oven. Wrap loosely in light cloth to cool. Serve warm if possible. Australians like scones with just plain butter when served hot. If served cool, they are the number one item for an afternoon tea. In this case, serve in wicker basket and allow guests to open cloth to retrieve scone. Provide whipped cream and a range of jellies and preserves for toppings, if guests are seated at table. Otherwise break scones in half (don't slice — don't ask why) and add toppings. Do not butter if you top with preserves and whipped cream.

VARIATIONS: Add 3 ounces of currants to the above mixture for delicious fruit scones. Alternatively, substitute 4 to 6 tablespoons of Parmesan cheese for the sugar to make tangy cheese scones.

Makes 12 scones.

ABOUT ELSIE: Elsie played tennis at her church until she was in her seventies. Thousands of Australians play team sports over the weekend in various church and local groups. Never has it been known for any of these matches (games) to run without a break for afternoon tea. (Well, this is a bit of an exaggeration.

They eat orange slices at three-quarter time in Aussie Rules football games, though we have it on good authority that some players do take a cup of tea at half time.) The scones in this recipe have fed hundreds of church-going tennis players.

CHEESE AND BACON SQUARES

1 sliced sandwich loaf
butter
1 cup grated cheddar cheese
½ pound lean bacon, lightly cooked
1 egg

- Trim crusts from bread slices, spread lightly with butter, and cut into squares. Mix cheese and egg well, then spoon onto bread. Place strips of bacon on top. Preheat oven to 375 degrees, place squares on cookie tray, and bake until golden brown, about 20 minutes. These are wonderful for breakfast ("brekkie" to Australians) and make impressive savories. Try freezing them and heat in a toaster oven for supper (that is, a bedtime snack.)

Makes 20 squares.

More confusion! We have never quite figured out how Americans refer to each of their daily meals. Is suppertime the same as dinnertime? And is it still dinner if you have it at midday? We always had Sunday dinner at home at midday. But we also had supper, as well as tea (that is, an evening meal). An Australian tradition when we were kids was to have supper (more for grown-ups than kids because it was usually indulged in after the kids were in bed) late in the evening, not too long before turning in. The most common food taken at this time would be a round or two of toast, and of course a cup of tea, and for the more indulgent, a little soup. A touch of Vegemite on the toast was also most welcome.

MAISIE'S CHEESE STRAWS

6 tablespoons butter
11 tablespoons self-rising flour
11 tablespoons grated extra sharp Cheddar cheese
sprinkle of cayenne pepper
flaked coconut

* Knead the butter, flour, cheese, and pepper together to make
  a pastry. Roll on a pastry sheet sprinkled with coconut and
  cut into straws about ½ inch wide and 3 inches long. Roll in
  more coconut. Bake on a tray in a 350-degree oven for about
  15 minutes. Take care not to burn the coconut. Cool on a wire
  rack and keep in an air-tight tin or container. Savory, crisp,
  and delicious with a predinner drink.

Makes 6 to 8 snacks.

PORTLAND RUSKS

This is a very old recipe (by Aussie standards)—at least three generations old, originating in the Portland area of Victoria, Australia's most southern state (excluding Tasmania). A rusk is a type of light, sweet cookie.

½ cup (1 stick) butter
½ cup fine sugar
1 egg
2 cups self-rising flour
pinch of salt
a little milk, if needed

- Cream butter and sugar, add beaten egg. Sift in flour and salt and knead well. Add milk if needed. Pat out to 1 inch thick and cut to desired size. Cook in 425-degree oven for 10 minutes. When cooked, break open with a fork and return to oven to dry out, for an additional 5 to 10 minutes. If using an electric oven, turn oven off, and use remaining heat in oven.

Makes 10 to 15 rusks.

ABOUT PORTLAND: The oldest settlement in Victoria, Portland was known to whalers for many years, but was officially settled in 1834. This town is situated on one of the most startling coastal roads in Australia.

Chapter 4

Shrimp, Snags, and Other Barbie Delights

The Australian barbecue (barbie) has become a great institution. It is by far the most popular way of cooking, especially when entertaining. The temperate climate makes it possible to spend a lot of time out of doors, which is where Australians like to be.

Get lots of steak, lamb chops (the little ones with the curly tails that cost a fortune in the United States, but are relatively cheap in Australia), snags (sausages), a gas barbecue, and plenty of beer, and you're set to entertain any number of easily satisfied guests.

Aussies sometimes have a BYO (bring your own) barbecue. This means that the host would provide the meat, and you would bring perhaps a salad or other dish. You might bring your own beer as well. In fact, according to the rules of drinking etiquette, you should bring at least one bottle of beer without being asked, to show that you're not bludging (living off) others.

Roasts are also very common in Australia, and these days are often cooked on the barbie. In the old days, of course, the roast was cooked every Sunday. Mom would put the roast in the oven, and it would be left to cook while we all went to church. However, we have included only one roast, that of roast lamb, because roasts are pretty much the same everywhere, and because we know that if we were to suggest to Americans that they roast their beef until it was very (and we mean *very*) well done, they would refuse to eat it. By and large, Australians, especially older Australians, tend to eat meat well done. There are, of course, many exceptions. Our Australian friends will probably attack us for this unkind observation. (Unkind, because it appears the common view in civilized countries of the Northern Hemisphere is that it is more cultured to eat meat rare. This view does not seem to take advantage of primitive man's discovery of fire.)

ABOUT AUSSIE BARBIES: Every person who claims to be a "true blue" Aussie (authentic Aussie) MUST have a barbie. These come in many different varieties, but probably the most popular are gas grills, the same as those found in the United States. Most public parks and recreational areas provide barbies for local use. These may be either gas or electric, and may be coin operated. Barbecues that rely on fires (charcoal, and even gas) are often not available because they are considered a fire risk in times of high fire danger.

QUEENSLAND GRILL

1 ½ pounds choice steak, cut into 4 slices
2 small bananas
½ cup medium-dry sherry
freshly ground pepper
4 slices fresh pineapple
4 tablespoons butter
1 tablespoon chopped fresh parsley

- Cut a pocket in each piece of steak and insert sliced banana. Pour a teaspoon of sherry in each, and close with a toothpick. Sprinkle with pepper and pour remaining sherry over top and allow to stand at least 4 hours in the refrigerator. Place steak under broiler and cook to desired doneness. Make parsley butter by beating butter, parsley, and a pinch of salt and pepper into a smooth paste. Just before serving, place pineapple slices on top and heat briefly. Remove toothpicks and top with parsley butter.

Serves 4.

NOTE: Trying to match American steaks to Australian steaks is very difficult. Australian butchers cut their meat differently from Americans. We have found through trial and error that a large London broil, as thick a piece as possible, comes very close to the Australian steak in this and other recipes. One can then cut the broil into the thickness desired for the particular recipe.

ABOUT QUEENSLAND: This state was named by Queen Victoria in 1859, and is often called the "Sunshine State." Today it is a tourist resort and an attractive place for retirement. Bushmen of Outback Queensland had a different view:

Queensland, thou art a land of pests!
From flies and fleas one never rests,

Even now mosquitoes 'round me revel,
In fact they are the very devil.
But bid thee now a long farewell,
Thou scorching sunburnt land of Hell!
   —*Bushman's Farewell to Queensland*, Anonymous, about 1870.

POCKET STEAK MELBOURNE

1 pound choice steak (2 pieces)
4 tablespoons butter
2 tablespoons finely chopped onion
1 cup sliced mushrooms
salt and pepper

Garlic butter:
1 clove garlic
salt and cayenne pepper
4 tablespoons butter

- Trim any excess fat from steak, and cut a pocket in each piece. Melt butter and sauté onion and mushrooms until onion is transparent. Season with salt and pepper, then fill each pocket with mixture, sealing with toothpick. Crush the garlic, add salt and cayenne and beat into butter until creamy. Brush steak with garlic butter, then salt and pepper, place steak under broiler. Quickly turn to other side and repeat procedure. Cook to desired doneness.
Serves 2 to 3.

ABOUT GARLIC: Among older Australians (in contrast to "new Australians" a term reserved by Australians of the 1950s for the thousands of immigrants who came to Australia after World War II under Australia's assisted immigration scheme) garlic has not been a popular ingredient, because it is thought to upset the stomach, or embarrass the diner with an odor that lingers on one's breath.

STEAK AND ONIONS

No country could lay claim to this dish as uniquely its own. Australia has its own version of this popular way to fix steak.

1 ½ pounds choice steak
1/3 cup flour
2 eggs, beaten
2 tablespoons milk
1 ½ cups bread crumbs
6 tablespoons butter
3 onions, sliced
salt and pepper

Choose a thick London broil for this dish, and cut it into thin slices. Dip each slice in flour, beaten eggs, and milk, then in bread crumbs. Coat each side well. Melt butter and lay steak on hot plate, or on grill covered with aluminum foil. On side or next to steak, sauté onions until golden brown. Season with salt and pepper. Cook steak to desired doneness, then serve smothered with onions.
Serves 4.

VARIATION: Cook your steak on a barbecue using a beer sauce.

BEER SAUCE

In a beer drinking country like Australia, what better sauce to baste your barbecue than one made of beer itself!

1 ½ cups tomato purée
1 can (12 ounces) beer
6 tablespoons Worcestershire sauce
¼ cup cider vinegar
1 teaspoon paprika
1 teaspoon salt
½ teaspoon pepper

- Combine all ingredients and heat to a simmer. Brush over meat every 5 minutes until meat has cooked.
Makes 3 cups.

VARIATIONS: If you are cooking lighter meats such as pork chops or chicken, use an ale or light beer. If red meats are to be basted, use a dark beer, or to avoid sweetness, use imported Guinness Stout. To baste lamb, substitute rosemary for the paprika, and use a light beer.

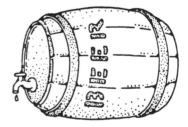

STEAK DIANNE

Steak Dianne is a universal favorite. One can hardly claim that it is an especially Australian dish. Yet, when one considers the early history of Australian foods—largely English in origin, which was to stick to plain and simple food, without any strong herbs or spices—Steak Dianne holds a special place. It was among the first of the more "spiced" or fancy dishes found acceptable by older Australians. These days, it is a popular item on many pub Counter Lunch menus.

1 ½ pounds choice steak
salt and pepper
4 tablespoons butter
1 clove garlic, finely chopped
¼ cup chopped parsley
2 tablespoons Worcestershire sauce

- Using meat mallet, pound steak until about 1 inch thick. Rub in salt and pepper. Bring butter to a sizzle, toss in meat and cook in hot pan 1 minute or less on each side. Turn back to first side, sprinkle with half the garlic and parsley and cook for 1 minute or less, then do same on other side. Add Worcestershire sauce and cook 1 minute more. Lift steak onto serving dish, cover with sauce from pan. Australians like this dish served with a crisp salad (on the same plate!).
Serves 4.

AUSTRALIAN MIXED GRILL

Because of the unavailability in the United States of one of the ingredients of this dish (snags), we can only approximate the Australian version of a mixed grill. The required ingredients are:

choice steak (rump or porterhouse)
snags (Aussie sausages)
loin lamb chops
bacon
large (preferably wild) mushrooms
butter
tomatoes, halved

- Whether grilled (broiled) or barbecued, this is a perennial favorite among Australians, still a nation of meat eaters, even though pasta and pizza have made quite a dent in Aussie food preferences.

- Broil steaks, snags, and lamb chops to the desired doneness. While meat is cooking, fry bacon to crisp, and sauté mushrooms in butter. When meat is almost cooked, place tomato halves under broiler and broil till sizzling. Turn out onto pre-warmed plates, placing bacon over lamb chop, and mushroom over steak. Australians like this dish with French fries (*chips* to Aussies).

ABOUT COOKING STEAK ON THE BARBIE: Not much to tell the experienced American barbecue cook. An expert Aussie barbie cook we know recommends that you paint each side of the steak with olive oil, make sure that the barbie is really hot, then lay the steak down on the grill, singeing each side quickly to seal in the juices. In the olden days basting with various sauces was not done, but in modern times, it is common.

Among certain hard-working individuals who like a big brekkie (breakfast), a mixed grill may find special attraction.

Unfortunately, we are unable to exactly replicate this recipe because there is no equivalent in America to snags. The closest we have found are sausage links, but these are usually way too spicy, the wrong shape, and don't have enough bread in them. Australian sausages come in two sizes. Short and fat (usually pork sausages), and long and thin (slightly longer than a regular hot dog). They are always strung together, and the butcher has to cut them off the string. Because the sausage meat is mixed with bread to form the sausage, such sausages simply do not exist in the United States—they would be illegal! But expatriate Aussies dream about them at least once a week.

GRILLED RUMP STEAK

By "grilled" we mean "broiled." Cook your steak in your favorite way. We prefer ours done over a barbecue. The special part of this recipe is the sauce.

1 ½ pounds rump steak
2 tablespoons butter
6 shallots, finely chopped
½ cup claret*
¾ cup tomato purée
salt and pepper
1 clove garlic
1 tablespoon chopped parsley

- Broil steak until done to your liking. Melt butter in pan and sauté shallots until tender. Add claret, purée, salt, pepper, and garlic. Stir until it boils and simmer for 5 minutes. Serve over steak and sprinkle with parsley. Serve with Joan's Pacific Salad, page 138.)
  Serves 4.

Rump steak is the more common, budget steak in Australia, most often featured on "Counter Lunches" which are low-priced meals that one can obtain in just about every pub. You won't get one in a pub with a sauce like this though. Our Australian friends who visit us in America mostly admit that American steak is better than Australian steak. We're not sure what "better" means. Australian steak is cut mainly from "range fed" beef. The difference in texture and taste is quite dramatic. American steak is more tender, and definitely sweeter.

*Any good dry red wine may be substituted, but for sentimental reasons, we'd be happier if you tried to obtain a bottle of Australian claret from your local liquor store.

ZUCCHINI BURGERS

1 pound lean minced steak
3 small (1 large) zucchini, grated
1 small onion, grated
1 teaspoon soy sauce
1 teaspoon grated ginger
1 egg yolk
hamburger buns
lettuce, tomato, and onion

- Combine first six ingredients. Shape into six patties (can be made smaller for small people). Barbecue or pan fry until done to your liking. Serve on toasted buns with salad. Lovely moist burger. Great for the barbecue.

Makes 6 burgers.

SEAFOOD SKEWERS WITH LIME DILL BUTTER

Lime dill butter:
2 egg yolks
1 teaspoon grated lime rind
2 tablespoons lime juice
½ cup (1 stick) butter
2 tablespoons chopped dill

2 pounds large shrimp
½ pound scallops
lime wedges (optional)
Sesame oil

If using bamboo skewers, soak well in water before threading seafood onto them.

For the lime dill butter, place egg yolks, rind and juice in a double boiler over hot water and whisk 1 minute. Chop butter into small pieces and whisk into the egg mixture. When sauce thickens remove from heat, stir in dill, and cool. Lime dill butter may be made 2 days ahead. Bring to room temperature before using.

Peel and devein shrimp, leaving tail intact. Thread shrimp, scallops, and lime wedges onto skewers. Brush with sesame oil and barbecue on a hot plate. Cook quickly and serve with dill butter.

Serves 6.

CHILI PRAWNS (SHRIMP) AND SCALLOPS

2 pounds green king prawns
1 pound scallops

Marinade:
1/3 cup oil
3 tablespoons honey
3 tablespoons chili sauce
2 tablespoons lemon juice
2 shallots, chopped
½ teaspoon five spice powder

- Shell prawns leaving tails intact, remove vein. Combine marinade ingredients in a bowl, mix well. Mix prawns and scallops into marinade and leave 1 to 2 hours in the refrigerator. Thread prawns and scallops onto skewers, threading the scallop in the curl of the prawn. Barbecue quickly. Brush with marinade during cooking. Do not overcook, 2 to 5 minutes should be enough. Use chili sauce to your taste. This is a "hot" marinade so use less chili and more lemon juice, if desired.

Serves 6.

NOEL'S BBQ BUGS RISQUE

2 fresh raw bugs (4 halves per serving)*
4 tablespoons butter
1 teaspoon chopped fresh ginger
rind and juice of 1 lemon
1 tablespoon finely chopped coriander

- Cut bugs in half lengthwise using extra strong kitchen shears; remove "mustard" and vein. Drain. Make herb butter by combining butter, ginger, lemon juice, and rind. Beat well and add coriander. Put into piping bag and pipe onto bug meat. Refrigerate for 30 minutes. Butter must be chilled for best results. Place bugs on a roasting rack, butter-side up. Place rack onto barbecue grill, close lid, and cook about 10 minutes. Cooking time will depend on the size of the bugs. Bugs may be baked in a hot oven instead of on the barbecue at 400 degrees for 10 minutes.

Serves 2.

*ABOUT BUGS: These strange creatures are definitely not insects! Bugs are a crustacean of ancient origin, similar to lobster in that all the meat is in the tail. The bug does not have any claws. In fact it looks a bit like a lobster without the claws. They are found in many of the bays along the eastern coast of Australia. The taste, we think, is a little more succulent than lobster. Obviously, for an American kitchen, lobster could be substituted for the bugs. And in case you're interested, bugs are just as expensive as lobsters ("crayfish" in Australia).

BARBIE ROAST LEG OF LAMB

We have included this recipe in the barbie section, even though most are used to cooking a roast in a standard oven in the kitchen. Aussies love their barbie so much that they quite often cook a roast in the barbie, lid-covered, of course.

1 leg of lamb (4 pounds)
oil (optional)
4 large potatoes peeled, cut in large chunks
4 whole medium onions, peeled
2 large carrots, cut in large chunks
2 large parsnips, cut in large chunks
½ pound pumpkin, cut in large chunks
½ pound fresh peas

Mint sauce:
2 tablespoons chopped fresh mint
¼ cup boiling water
2 tablespoons sugar
06[Alt+0190] cup vinegar

- Start barbie on low heat, cover down. Depending on the type of lamb, you may need to paint the lamb with oil. Australian lamb usually does not require it. Allow 25 minutes per pound of meat. Check and turn every 15 to 20 minutes. Of course, if you have a spit on your barbie, this is by far the best way to roast the lamb. In this case, the lid may be left off. Parboil potatoes, onions, carrots, parsnips, and pumpkin and add to hot plate of barbie about ½ hour before serving. Lightly boil peas.

TO PREPARE THE MINT SAUCE: Wash and dry the mint; finely chop. Pour over boiling water, add sugar and stir until dissolved. Add vinegar, stir. Serve in small jug with teaspoon.

Remove roast from barbie. Carve thin slices of lamb, place on preheated plates. Carefully arrange selection of barbie-roasted vegetables on each person's plate. Add spoonful of peas to each serving. Bring each plate to guests seated at dining table. Pass around rich brown gravy and mint sauce.

Serves 6 to 8.

ABOUT THE AUSTRALIAN ROAST: Lamb is the "flagship" meat of Australia. It has been the tradition in many Australian families to eat a roast dinner, usually roast lamb (but roast mutton or beef is also common) every Sunday, usually after coming home from church. We have described here the traditional way of serving the roast, which is to prepare each individual diner's plate in advance, with each prepared plate brought to the diner at the table, as in a restaurant. In modern times, it is more likely that the various dishes would be passed around for each to take his or her portion, as is the common practice in America. The modern practice is particularly so when the roast lamb is cooked on top of the barbie.

Chapter 5

Fish, Chook, and Rabbit

*A*ustralia has an enormous coastline because it is both a
continent and an island. One would expect a nation of
fishermen and fish eaters. This is not the case. Instead, Australia has been, until very recently, a nation of sheep, cattle, and
wheat farmers. The bulk of the population in the cities ate the
foods they produced.

Today, it is the frontier of the 90s, with new mining towns
opening up in outback regions, and industrial suburbs cropping
up everywhere. Fish consumption has not increased particularly,
though that perennial favorite, fish and chips, has steadfastly
withstood the onslaught of American fast-food chains. More
chooks (chickens) are eaten, though, because of increased mass
farming and marketing of chickens. Although there are many
homes with chooks in the backyard, very few of these families
would kill their own chooks for the table. It's easier to buy them,
after all. Backyard chooks are kept mainly for their eggs.

Rabbit is a fading food, though more prevalent than in America. Come to think of it, we have never seen rabbit on the menu
of any American restaurant, or in any food store. Our guess is
that if it did appear, it would be considered a gourmet item. The
reasons for the demise of rabbit as a common Australian food are
many, some of which we'd rather not write about. The Australian
government has sponsored many different attempts to reduce the

rabbit population. Though it is still done, not so many people catch their own rabbits any more.

More importantly, rabbit has become less popular because chicken has become more widely available. On the few occasions we went to restaurants as kids, we remember the grown-ups joking about whether a dish presented as chicken, really was chicken, and not rabbit in disguise. Rabbit was much cheaper and more widely available in the old days. We will have more to say about rabbits later. They are definitely part of the Australian folklore.

Aussie Chips (French Fries)

Fish and Chips are represented to Americans as an English invention, which we are prepared to admit, though grudgingly so. However, just as spaghetti has been reinvented by a number of cultures (China, Italy, and America to name but a few), so have chips or French fries. The fact is that French fries taste different everywhere, even in fast-food restaurants. There are important reasons for this, and important eating traditions that go along with these different types of French fries.

In Australia there are shops devoted entirely to selling fish and chips. While some of these shops might provide seating, it is generally expected that you will take your fish and chips out.

There are probably no fish and chip shops in Australia that are owned or run by Pommies (i.e. English). They are invariably owned by what were called in the 1950s, "new Australians,"— Australia's more recent immigrants, generally of Mediterranean origin.

True Aussie chips are not as crisp or thin as the French fries sold in certain American fast-food restaurants (now all over Australia). The potatoes in those French fries have been frozen, and for potatoes to be frozen they have to be a special kind of potato that is low in water content. Their taste is, if you'll forgive us, sterile although the texture is acceptable.

Dinkum (authentic) Aussie chips are partially fried a day or two ahead of time. If you visit a fish and chips shop, you will see mounds of these partially cooked chips. This has the effect of changing the consistency of the potato to a much smoother, less powdery texture. This (along with the particular oil used for deep frying), conserves the potato flavor. When you ask for "a dollar's worth of chips," the cook will scoop some up and deep fry them in a matter of minutes. He will then (if it is a true, traditional fish and chip shop) wrap these chips, along with their fish, in thick paper. This has the effect of making sure that nothing inside could remain crisp. Instead, the chips become soft and soggy, but also remain very hot for a long time. Kids buy these, tear a whole in the top, and pull out one chip at a time. The chips are about three times fatter than French fries bought in America. Years ago, before nuisance health regulations, fish and chips were wrapped in one layer of white paper, then in newspaper.

In any season, there's nothing like a pack of hot fish and chips with plenty of salt, and a cold bottle of beer!

FISH AND CHIPS

½ pound fish fillets
½ cup flour
1 pinch salt
1 teaspoon cooking oil
2 eggs
1 ¼ cups warm water
4 large potatoes, peeled and diced for French fries (chips)
cooking oil for French fries (chips)
cooking oil for fish fry

- Sift flour and salt together and make into a mound. Make a hole in center and pour oil in, then stir with a wooden spoon, adding water slowly. Mix until a smooth paste is obtained. Separate whites from eggs and beat to a stiff froth, fold lightly into flour mixture. Discard egg yolks. Wipe fish fillets dry with paper towel, dip in flour, then into batter. Heat oil in pan, add fish and cook briskly until golden brown.

FOR THE CHIPS (French fries): Dice potatoes into desired shapes. Wipe off excess moisture with paper towel, fry in fresh, hot oil. (See Aussie Chips, page 70)

Serve fish and chips with slice of lemon, salt, and a crisp salad (on same plate) of lettuce and tomato. Vinegar is very popular for the fish. *Never*, repeat, *never* pour ketchup on your chips. This is an American influence strongly resisted by true-blue Aussies!

Serves 4.

ABOUT FISH FILLETS IN AUSTRALIA: The fish used for fish and chips varies depending on the region in Australia. In southern Victoria, whiting is the clear favorite. Whiting are the most popular fish served in pub Counter Lunches, although a fish called "flathead," bountiful in the bays and coastal inlets of Australia, is also popular. In Queensland (Australia's Florida), a reef fish such as sea perch or coral trout would be a favorite.

In America, frozen whiting is probably the best fish to use, although it does not have the rich taste of Australian whiting. In days gone by, if you bought fish and chips at an Australian fish and chip shop, and did not specify the fish, you would have received the cheapest fish called "flake." This is actually shark, and it's delicious, tender, and flaky (hence its name). Unfortunately, in parts of Australia, shark is not as popular because some of it has a high mercury content.

GRILLED (BROILED) FLOUNDER

Whole flounder
Parsley butter (page 53)

- Select large, whole flounder. Flounder is fresh if the eyes are prominent and bright, the flesh is firm, and it has an agreeable smell. If in doubt, don't buy it. Do not use this recipe for flounder fillets.

Wash flounder well, remove head if desired. It is unnecessary to skin this fish. The flounder is a flat fish with both eyes on one side of its body. Turn over so that underside (usually white in color) faces up and paint liberally with parsley butter. Place under broiler and cook for 5 minutes or until browning occurs. Remove, turn over carefully so that cooked flesh does not break, and repeat process for top side (usually dark in color). Cook until brown. Serve on large oval plate with chips (French fries), garnished with crisp salad of lettuce and tomato, and slice of lemon.

HOW TO EAT IT: Grilled whole flounder is a popular Counter Lunch item. Australians like them so that they cover almost an entire oval-shaped plate. A simple trick will make eating flounder more enjoyable. Begin by eating first one side, then turn the flounder completely over and eat the other side. Taking a little more care with the fin area, this method makes the flounder an easy fish to eat without too much worry about loose bones. Whole flounder tastes completely different from the flounder fillets one finds in America. The meat is richer in flavor, and the texture is more flaky, and less stringy. When we were very young, flounder could be speared in the shallow waters of Corio Bay (just near Melbourne), right in the heart of industrial areas. We would take a long pole with a small light attached on the end, and a spear about 5 feet long. The flounder are attracted to light (the dark early morning hours are the favorite times to fish) and when they come up close, they can be speared. Alas, pollution and overfishing has eliminated the possibility of doing this any more.

CRAYFISH SALAD

large crayfish (steamed)
Sydney rock oysters
cooked medium shrimp
deep-fried Tasmanian scallops (cold)
lemon slices, halved
fresh garden vegetables for salad

* Break open the crayfish by slicing down the middle of the back. Scoop out meat. Arrange crayfish on lettuce leaves with legs and shells for decoration, surrounded with scallops and/or shrimp. Place Sydney rock oysters (raw and on the shell) with half slices of lemon around plate. Add firm slices of tomato, celery sticks, orange slices carrot sticks to plate. Provide a small jar of cocktail sauce and small jar of paste from head of the crayfish (called "mustard" because it looks like mustard). Serve with fresh fingers of white bread and butter. A delicious, dry Australian white wine would be most appropriate. For a special treat, try the oysters with a small glass of very dry sherry.

ABOUT CRAYFISH: Crayfish are the Australian equivalent (almost) of the lobster. In fact their tails are airlifted to some American restaurants and sold as lobster. The crayfish is found in most ocean waters of Australia, though those we are most familiar with are taken from the cooler ocean waters in the southern tip of Australia, near Bass Straight (the strip of water that separates continental Australia from its sixth state, Tasmania). Crayfish do not have the huge pincers that lobsters from North America have. Their shells tend to be very rough and jagged, and the pincers are longer and narrower. To make up for this, the rest of the legs of the crayfish probably have a little more meat in them than the lobster. They are just as expensive as their North American cousins.

BATTER-FRIED GOODIES (POTATO CAKES 1)

½ teaspoon salt
1 ½ cups self-rising flour
½ teaspoon pepper
2 tablespoons butter
½ pound boiled potatoes
milk to moisten
oil for frying

- Sift dry ingredients together and rub in butter. Mash potatoes well. Mix with flour and milk to make a stiff dough. Roll out and cut into rounds about ½ inch thick. Fry in hot pan until brown on both sides.
Makes 6 servings.

BATTER-FRIED GOODIES (POTATO CAKES 2)

½ pound potatoes, peeled
batter (from Fish and Chips, page 72)
oil for frying

- Parboil potatoes. Remove, drain, and allow to cool sufficiently to cut into slices about 1 inch thick. Dip each slice in batter, then fry in hot oil until golden brown on each side.
Makes 6 servings.

RICE FRITTERS

2 eggs
1 cup boiled rice
2 teaspoons finely chopped parsley
salt and pepper
batter (from Fish and Chips, page 72)
oil for frying
spaghetti sauce (optional)

- Beat eggs well, add rice, parsley, salt and pepper: mix well then mold into patties. Dip in batter and fry in hot pan until golden brown. Serve with warm spaghetti sauce.

VARIATION: Substitute 1 to 2 tablespoons finely chopped pineapple for parsley.
Serves 4.

SEAFOOD PIE

Crust:
1 cup crushed crackers
¼ cup water
6 tablespoons butter, melted

- Combine all ingredients until stiff dough is formed, then press into a 9-inch pie pan. Chill.

Filling:
2 tablespoons celery powder
1 onion, chopped
oil
3 eggs
1 cup milk
1 can cream of oyster soup
1 cup small shrimp
2 tablespoons celery powder

- Sauté onion in a little oil, stir in soup. Remove from heat. Beat eggs and milk, add to soup mixture. Stir in shrimp and celery powder, and spoon carefully into pie crust. Bake at 300 degrees for 40 to 50 minutes.
Serves 4.

ABOUT CANNED SOUP: Australian families have very busy schedules, just like American families. Over the past 15 years or so, the number of families with both husband and wife working has increased at about the same rapid rate as in the United States. Quick meals have become the order of the day, and ready-made soups (the most common brand is Heinz) make these and some other meals in this chapter possible.

FISH CASSEROLE

1 pound cooked smoked cod
1 small onion, sliced
4 tablespoons butter
2 hard-boiled eggs
1 cup cooked peas
1 small can sweet corn
bread crumbs for topping

Sauce:
4 tablespoons butter
4 tablespoons flour
cayenne pepper
1 ¼ cups milk

- Bone and flake cod and remove skin. Sauté onion in 4 tablespoons of butter and set aside. Make sauce by melting 4 tablespoons butter. Stir in flour and cayenne, and cook for 1 minute. Gradually add milk, stirring until thick. Fold in all other ingredients, cod last so that it does not break up. Spoon into casserole and sprinkle with bread crumbs. Bake in 350-degree oven until hot and topping is crisp, about 30 minutes.

Serves 6.

SWEET AND SOUR FISH

2 ½ tablespoons butter
1 cup flour
1 cup cooked peas
2 cups chopped celery
1 ¼ cups milk
1 cup white vinegar
1 cup sugar
2 cans (6 ounces each) tuna
1 cup (or less) cooked rice

- Melt butter in pan, add flour and mix to paste. On moderate heat, add milk slowly, stirring until sauce thickens. Add vinegar and sugar, mix well. Fold in tuna, peas, and celery and gradually add cooked rice, using less rice if mixture is stiff. Place in greased casserole and bake in 300-degree oven until hot, about 30 minutes. Serve with fluffy boiled rice.
Serves 4.

PERTH PIE

3 tablespoons butter
¼ cup flour
1 ¼ cups milk
½ tablespoon mayonnaise
1 beaten egg
¼ lemon for juice
1 can (14 ounces) salmon

- Make a Mornay sauce by melting butter in pan, add flour and mix into paste. On moderate heat, add milk slowly, stirring until sauce thickens. Mix mayonnaise, beaten egg, and lemon juice together and add a small amount of the white sauce, stirring continually. Return this mixture to the rest of the sauce and heat well. Drain salmon and fold into mixture. Use juice from salmon instead of milk if stronger flavor is desired. Turn into a casserole.

Crust:
2 cups self-rising flour
2 tablespoons butter
milk
grated sharp cheese
cayenne pepper

- Rub butter into flour until flour looks like oatmeal. Add milk and work until dough is soft. Roll out into oblong shape and sprinkle with grated cheese. Add cayenne pepper to taste. Cut into 1-inch pieces and place on top of casserole with cut side up. Bake in 400-degree oven until dough on top is golden brown.
Serves 4.

ABOUT PERTH. Perth is the capital of Australia's largest state, Western Australia. It is named after the city of the same name in Scotland. What similarity the British saw between the two places is puzzling indeed. They have nothing in common, but do have a big difference: the sun. We Australians tend to believe that, just as many Aussies have never seen snow, many British have never seen the sun! Perth is the sunniest city in Australia, with an incredible average daily sunshine of 7.8 hours.

SHOOTERS (for adults only)

½ dozen fresh oysters
shot glasses
vodka (may be frozen)
tomato juice

* Details of the method we leave to the self control of our readers! Place one fresh oyster in a shot glass, cover with vodka and tomato juice, and down it! It would be sensible to eat a little bread with each one. Six of these and you better not stand up, let alone drive! This appetizer is definitely not for underage drinkers. The drinking age for Aussie youth is 18.

CHICKEN CAIRNS SUPREME

2 pounds chicken pieces
½ cup flour
2 slices bacon
1 large onion, chopped
4 tablespoons butter
1 can (14 ½ ounces) cream of chicken soup
1 cup chopped celery
4 tablespoons cream
toasted almonds

- Remove skin from chicken and dust with flour. Fry bacon and onion in butter until cooked but not brown. Arrange chicken pieces in casserole dish. Cover with bacon and onion and can of soup. Cover, heat oven to 400 degrees, and bake 35 minutes. Mix together celery and cream, pour on casserole, and top with toasted almonds. Bake an additional 10 to 15 minutes.

VARIATION: Chicken or turkey leftovers may be used in this recipe. In this case, simply arrange leftovers in casserole, cover with soup, bacon, and sautéed onion, and heat in a 400-degree oven for 30 minutes. Add celery and cream before serving.

ABOUT CAIRNS: Cairns is a large tourist city in the north of Queensland, gateway to the Great Barrier Reef, a coral reef of spectacular beauty, and thousands of miles long. The city was established in 1873 and named after the governor of Queensland (1875-1877), Sir William Wellington Cairns. It is a city of particular interest to older Australians and to Americans of similar vintage, for it was here that there was an important air base during World War II. Old Australians still remember the American presence in Australia and the Pacific during World War II. The Coral Sea Battle was commemorated every year when we went to school in Australia. Many Australians felt then—we're not sure whether this feeling continues today—that had it not been for the "Yanks" (a term of endearment as used by Aussies), Australia would have suffered badly in World War II. It was widely believed that the Americans saved Australia from a Japanese invasion. Thank you, America!

CHICKEN PIE

2 ½ pounds chicken
1 onion, cut in pieces
2 carrots
bay leaves
2 stems parsley
whole black peppercorns
6 tablespoons butter
3 slices bacon
1 cup flour
freshly ground pepper
salt
1 recipe pastry (see Maisie's Pasties, page 20)

- Place chicken in pot with vegetables, bay leaves, parsley, peppercorns, and about 2 inches of water. Bring to boil and simmer for about 1 hour. Strain off liquid and make up to 1 ¼ cups with water if necessary. Discard vegetables and herbs. Skin chicken and carve flesh into thick slices, removing all meat from bones. Melt butter and fry bacon, set aside. Add flour to butter left in pan and cook for 2 minutes. Add reserved liquid, stirring constantly until it comes to boil, then cook for 2 minutes. Season with freshly ground black pepper, and salt to taste. Add carved chicken and bacon, cover, and allow to cool.

While it is cooling, make the pastry and roll it out. Line large pie pan and pour chicken filling in pastry. Cover with pastry, and decorate with strips of pastry trimmed from edge, made into a lattice. Brush with beaten egg and cook in a 375-degree oven for 1 hour. Can be eaten hot or cold.

Makes one 10-inch pie.

ABOUT CHICKEN: Chicken is not as widely eaten in Australia as in the United States, although it is becoming more and more popular. In our opinion, it costs more than it does in America. When we were kids, chicken was served as a real delicacy, usually on a special occasion. Turkey was unheard of. In fact one of us had never eaten turkey until coming to the United States. Chicken pies are not all that common. Certainly, they're no match for Aussie meat pies. One rarely sees chicken pies on sale in the store.

CHICKEN MARYLAND

chicken
½ cup seasoned flour
2 eggs (more if needed)
2 cups bread crumbs (more if needed)
oil for frying
2 potatoes
½ cup sweet corn
2 bananas

- Cut chicken into sections and parboil. When cold, roll in seasoned flour, egg, and bread crumbs. Fry in oil until cooked and outside is crisp and golden, about 15 minutes. Cook potatoes and mash well, bind with sweet corn to make patties, then roll in egg and bread crumbs. Cut bananas into four and roll in egg and bread crumbs. Fry bananas and corn patties until golden brown.

Sauce:
4 tomatoes
½ onion
1 piece of bacon *or* 1 teaspoon cooking oil
2 ½ cups beef bouillon
ham bone
salt and pepper
1 ½ teaspoons cornstarch
soy sauce (optional)

- Dice tomatoes, chop onion finely. Heat oil and sauté onion until transparent, add tomatoes and cook 5 minutes. Add bouillon, ham bone, salt and pepper, and simmer 1 hour. Remove from heat and purée. Blend cornstarch with a little water, then add to mixture. Stir well and cook another 2 minutes. Color and flavor with soy sauce, if desired. Serve chicken pieces on large platter, with banana and corn arranged between pieces. Pipe mashed potato around edge of platter. Pour sauce over chicken.

VARIATIONS: Substitute pineapple pieces or apple slices for the sweet corn. Instead of frying as above, dip chicken and accompaniments in batter (see Fish and Chips, page 72) and deep fry.
Serves 4 to 6.

This can't be Australian! Chicken Maryland is no doubt an American dish. Yet this is one of the oldest chicken recipes one will find in Australia. It is also very popular, and will be found on most menus of better pubs that offer a Counter Lunch a cut above the usual. The established popularity of this dish is all the more puzzling given that Australians, by comparison to Americans, do not eat a lot of chicken and rarely eat sweet corn. Come to think of it, apple or pineapple are more often than not substituted for corn. Only very recently have we seen fresh corn (called "maize" by Australians) at the green grocer (vegetable store).

ABOUT CHOOKS: We have no idea why chickens are called "chooks" in Australia. Keeping a few chooks in the backyard is a fairly common practice. They don't cost too much to feed, they eat many of the nuisance pests (grubs) in the garden, their dung (in limited quantities) may be used for fertilizer, and they are a source of a few fresh eggs each day. Chooks also contribute to the rich sounds of Australian suburbia. Their constant clucking is a comforting sound heard when one wanders through the fence-lined suburbs of city and small town alike. The day's sounds begin early with the cries of roosters from the backyards of hundreds of houses, and the warbling of magpies from the tops of lampposts. In smaller towns, one is sure to hear kookaburras cackling in the evening.

APRICOT CHICKEN

1 ½ pounds chicken pieces
1 cup apricot nectar (juice)
1 packet French onion soup
10 dried apricots

- Place chicken into a shallow casserole. Sprinkle soup powder over the pieces, then pour on apricot juice. Cook in a 325-degree oven for 50 minutes. Add chopped dried apricots and cook an additional 10 minutes.

Serves 4 to 6.

CHINESE FOWL

1 (1 ½ pound) chicken
2 tablespoons soy sauce
6 small mushrooms
2 tablespoons Chinese gin
½ teaspoon sugar
2 cups chopped Chinese sausages
2 Chinese pickled cucumbers, chopped
¼ teaspoon allspice
¼ teaspoon ginger

Rub fowl all over with soy sauce. Mix all ingredients and stuff chicken. Roast in oven 1 to 2 hours, depending on size of chicken. For an added treat, peel and slice potatoes as for French fries. Rub all over with soy sauce, fry lightly, add to chicken 30 minutes before serving.
Serves 4 to 6.

Chinese Australian? You betcha! There is an old and well established Chinese community in Australia. Most of them came to Australia during the gold rush of 1851. Others, though, were imported for cheap labor in Australia's sugar cane state, Queensland, also in the nineteenth century. Before the tremendous immigration after World War II of European and Mediterranean peoples who brought with them wonderful cooking traditions, Chinese food was widely established. "Dim sims" (dim sum in America) can be bought as take-out food almost everywhere.

Celestial is the way he works
The frying-pan and pot.
A splendid feed can be produced
While you'd be counting three,
By the Mandarin from China
That keeps company with me.
—*The Mandarin from China* by Alexander Forbes, 1869

RAGOUT OF RABBIT

1 rabbit
2 tablespoons flour
1 teaspoon salt
pepper
1 onion
2 tablespoons oil
2 cups water
mixed herbs
1 slice bacon

- Wash rabbit in warm water and cut into sections. Roll in flour, pepper, and salt. Heat oil in pan, then fry rabbit on high heat, both sides. Set rabbit aside. Peel and slice onion. Place onion in pan and fry with flour that remains. When brown, add water, herbs, and bacon. Bring to boil, add rabbit then simmer for 1 ½ hours.

Serves 4.

TO SKIN A RABBIT: See page 255. In Australia it is possible to buy rabbits frozen, whole or cut-up. Rabbit should be soaked in salt water for about 11 hours before cooking, to ensure that it is thoroughly clean. After soaking, wash with clean water, and cut off tail and a little of the backbone. Many rabbit dishes use bacon. This is not to mask the flavor (which is succulent, and similar to chicken, if properly cooked), but to make up for the extreme leanness of rabbit flesh. It is a healthy meat, by all accounts.

DANDENONG RABBIT PIE

If you would like to eat rabbit but pretend that it's chicken, then this is the dish for you.

1 boiled rabbit
3 tablespoons butter
5 tablespoons flour
¾ cup evaporated milk
1 ½ cups chicken broth
1 cup diced carrot
1 cup cooked peas
6 small white onions
salt and pepper
½ cup bread crumbs
grated cheddar cheese

• Prepare rabbit according to instructions in Ragout Rabbit, see page 91. Cut meat into small pieces. Make a white sauce: melt the butter and add the flour to make a paste. Over medium heat, gradually add evaporated milk and broth, stirring until thick. Fold in meat, carrot, peas, and onions. Season with salt and pepper. Fill ovenproof dish. Cover with bread crumbs and cheese. Brown under broiler, then bake in 400-degree oven for 20 to 25 minutes.

Serves 4.

ABOUT RABBIT: Rabbits are yet another gift from the English who settled Australia. When we were kids, there were so many of them that rabbits almost ate Australia. Many methods were used to reduce their population. One was to conduct a "rabbit drive." We remember one such drive, organized by a local church group, in which we began on a cockey's (farmer's) property, forming a long line of people, and made lots of noise. All the rabbits ran ahead of us, and were captured in a corner of the paddock surrounded by a rabbitproof fence. There were hundreds of rabbits hanging over the fence. Who ate all those rabbits is still a puzzle. We do not know many Australians who ate rabbit on a regular basis. In fact the only place that regularly served rabbit, in our experience, was the dorm one of us stayed in during college. Guess that figures!

RABBIT MUSHROOM CASSEROLE

1 rabbit
4 tablespoons butter
salt and pepper
1 tablespoon flour
4 ounces bacon
1 cup chicken broth
2 tablespoons tomato paste
½ cup sliced mushrooms
¼ cup grated Parmesan cheese
1 tablespoon chopped parsley

- Cut rabbit into serving portions. Melt butter in a pan. Roll rabbit pieces in salt, pepper and flour. Fry in butter until brown on both sides. Allow to cool, then wrap each piece in bacon, securing with a toothpick. Empty into casserole, add chicken broth, tomato paste, and mushrooms. Cook in 350-degree oven for 2 hours. If needed, thicken juice with a little cornstarch or arrowroot. Serve topped with grated cheese and parsley.

Serves 4.

ABOUT RABBITS. As cute as rabbits are, they have been a serious pest just about everywhere in Australia. They have competed for a limited amount of grass with Australia's sheep (who have traditionally had first priority), not to mention Australia's indigenous grass eaters, the kangaroos. There are also hares in Australia, though not so many (see jugged hare, page 255). These tend to be much larger than the common gray rabbit, and are usually more tan in color.

We also went rabbiting with ferrets, ferocious little beasts. As kids, our job was to locate all the exits of the rabbit burrow. All but two would be blocked up. The ferret was put down one, and we waited at the other end for the rabbits to dash out, going at high speed. The challenge was not only to catch the rabbit in a net, but to catch the ferret bent on destruction of its prey, and avoid getting bitten (by the ferret).

Chapter 6

The Aussie Melting Pot

*A*ustralia, the Timeless Land is not timeless when it comes to eating. The eating habits of Australians changing rapidly. In the first edition of this book we noted that Australia had become a melting pot, with the wide variety of immigrants who had come to Australia during the latter part of the 1800s and most of the twentieth century. However, perhaps the period of most rapid change, in regards to eating has been the last 10 years, with the influx of a wider variety of Asian peoples into Australia, and the final acceptance (perhaps an understatement—certainly an acceptance with open arms) of Italian pasta and pizza. While Chinese cuisine has been known to Australians since the Gold Rush days of the nineteenth century, Italian cuisine appeared on the Australian scene more recently. It took probably a generation until Italian cooking caught on in Australia. People of our parents' generation are probably still not especially keen on pasta. But our generation is very much at home with it, and of course our kids eat virtually nothing else (except breakfast cereal!).

The Australian continent is about the same size as the continental United States, yet its population is only 18 million. Australia's scarce resource is people, and successive governments have responded to this scarcity by well orchestrated immigration programs. Today, there is a tremendous variety of people living in Australia's cities. In fact, Melbourne (capital of the state of Victoria) is the third largest Greek-speaking city in the world. The influence on Australia's restaurants, therefore, by people from the Mediterranean, and more recently from parts of the Pacific Islands and Southeast Asia, is considerable. It is only a matter of time until the cooking traditions of these countries seep into the traditional Australian kitchens. In the first edition of this book, a conscious effort was made to minimize the number of recipes of recent immigrant origin, since we hoped to preserve the older Australian tradition of cooking. But in the 10 years since the first edition of this book, it has become more and more clear that the recent Asian, Pacific, and European influence on Australia has become part of the Australian homecooking tradition. We have, therefore, included in this chapter recipes in which these cultures' influence is clearly identifiable. We are sure these recipes have become regular favorites in the modern Australian kitchen.

We have also included vegetarian dishes in this chapter. Only 10 years ago, such dishes would have been very rare in Australia, a nation of meat eaters. However, influence from the United States and other parts of the world, particularly in regard to health choices and the campaigning of animal rights, has made vegetarian eating now more or less acceptable in Aussieland.

Also included in this chapter are stews, casseroles, and curries (both meat and meatless) all of which nestle very well into Australia's traditional way of life because they allow for an informal eating style. By this we mean that they are most often cooked for occasions when there are large family get-togethers, or for social gatherings, where the casserole can be placed at center table, and dinner served in "smorgasbord" fashion. If presented in this way, they provide no difficulty for the American guest. But should they be served in a formal, sit-down dinner style, then the American guest may be in for a bit of a problem. In fact, any formal dinner makes for a problem for Americans eating in Australia.

The reason is that Americans don't hold their knife and fork properly. In an informal smorgasbord style, the American way of eating a casserole-type dish, using the fork in one's dominant hand and collecting the food onto the concave surface of the fork is quite all right. But in a formal dinner, this is unacceptable because the knife must be held in the right hand (whether dominant or not) and the fork in the left. To make matters even more difficult, the fork must be held with the concave side down which means that there is a definite limit on how much food one can heap onto the fork.

Managing a plate full of casserole and vegetables requires a lot of practice. However, in some respects, casseroles are a good place to start, because usually there is enough food with some body or absorbent texture (potatoes are very useful). One can push food that might normally fall off on onto the fork (peas, for example), first into the potato, then onto the fork.

Learning to use a knife and fork is also easier with a casserole-type food because no cutting is required. Here is where Americans are often unfairly maligned. They have been observed holding the fork gripped in the palm of their hand, as though they were about to use it in an Agatha Christie murder scene! The fork must be held in the left hand, pointer finger running down on top of the fork handle, thumb to the side, other fingers curled around and under. The end of the fork pushes up against the palm of the hand. The concave side of the fork is always facing down. It takes a lot of practice to cut steak like this. We suggest you do it somewhere away from others, because we have seen a whole chop accidentally flipped across the width of a dining table when an unfortunate diner's pointer finger slipped off the knife handle!

The drawbacks to eating a casserole with a knife and fork are the juice and gravy. Fortunately, Australians don't mind if you use bread (spread with butter, of course) to soak up the remaining gravy. You might even get away with mopping up the gravy with bread held in hand. The more acceptable way would be to place the entire slice of bread and butter on your dinner plate, then cut it up into small pieces with your knife and fork.

We might add that we have noted, as a sign of decadence in Australian society, a definite tendency on the part of young Aussies (and even older ones) to use the fork in the right hand, very much in American style, especially when eating rice and other Asian-style stir-fries, or when eating spaghetti. We assume that this sign of decadence is a result of the slow but sure influx of Italian pastas and Asian stir-fries into the Aussie menu. We do understand the necessity for these changes. If you have tried to eat spaghetti with a knife and fork held in the "correct" manner, you will understand how difficult it is!

The old ways and traditions are quickly disappearing. It is claimed that three quarters of the children of immigrants in Australia marry outside their own culture. In the 1950s, 80 percent of the population was white European, largely of English stock. It is expected that by the turn of the century, over half of Australia's population will be from cultures other than Anglo-Saxon. New cooking traditions will arise, and many old traditions will be adapted to new tastes. So this chapter has a blend of old and new, but even with old recipes, we see the influence of other cultures. Strictly speaking, Australia is a land made up totally of immigrants, if we include in these our forefathers who came from England over the last two centuries. And there have been many different cultural groups who have found their way to Australia's shores over that time.

JACKEROO CHOPS

2 pounds lamb chops
2 tablespoons flour
1 teaspoon sugar
salt and pepper
6 tablespoons ketchup
4 tablespoons Worcestershire sauce
2 tablespoons vinegar
1 cup water

- Remove fat from chops, roll in flour with sugar, salt, and
  pepper. Combine ketchup, Worcestershire, vinegar, and
  water and pour over meat. Bake 1 hour at 375 degrees.
Serves 4 to 5.

JACKEROO: A jackeroo is a station hand, usually on a large
station in the outback. In folk poetry, he is often of "good
breeding" and lives with the station hands in order to gain
experience:

When you get on to the station, of small things you'll make a
    fuss,
And in speaking of the station, mind, it's we, and ours, and us.
Boast of your grand connections and your rich relations, too,
And your own great expectations, Jimmy Sago, Jackeroo.

When the boss wants information, on the men y'll do a sneak,
And don a paper collar on your fifteen bob a week*.
Then at the lamb-marking a boss they'll make of you
Oh that's the way to get on, Jimmy Sago, Jackeroo!
—*Jimmy Sago, Jackeroo, Anonymous*

*"bob" is slang for "shillings" used long before Australia
changed to decimal currency; worth about $1.50

GLAZED PORK FILLETS

¼ cup tomato sauce
¼ cup honey
2 teaspoons soy sauce
¼ teaspoon five-spice powder
¼ teaspoon crushed garlic
4 pork fillets

- Combine all the ingredients, except pork, and warm in a microwave for 30 seconds. Mix well then pour over the pork fillets in a glass dish. Let stand for 1 hour in refrigerator. Barbecue or oven bake at 400 degrees until the desired level of doneness. Glaze may be brushed on meat during cooking. This glaze can be kept in the refrigerator in a sealed container for up to a week and used on other pork cuts, such as chops, ham steaks, or ribs.

Serves 4.

ABOUT FIVE-SPICE POWDER: Used in much oriental cooking, this powder is made up of star anise, cinnamon, cloves, fennel and pepper, and has a distinctive, but mild aniseed flavor.

APRICOT PORK CHOPS

½ cup dried apricots
1 cup water
1 shallot, chopped
½ cup white vinegar
1/3 cup honey
¼ cup ketchup
½ teaspoon soy sauce
2 tablespoons oil
4 pork chops

- Combine apricots and water in a pan and bring to boil. Reduce heat, and simmer until tender, 15 minutes. Put apricots into the blender, blend until smooth. Return apricots to pan with other ingredients. Bring to a boil, reduce heat, and simmer for 5 minutes. Barbecue pork chops or bake in oven at 400 degrees until well done. Add sauce to meat at serving time, or brush on during cooking. Apricot sauce keeps very well in the refrigerator in a screw-topped jar for up to one month. Great on chicken too. Delicious hot or cold.

Makes 2 cups.

FRUIT CHOPS MILDURA

6 pork loin chops
salt and pepper
½ cup pineapple juice
½ cup honey
¼ cup brown sugar
1 teaspoon mustard (optional)
4 to 6 whole cloves
6 slices of orange
6 slices of lemon
6 maraschino cherries

- Brown chops on both sides in buttered pan until almost cooked, add salt and pepper. Combine pineapple juice, honey, brown sugar, mustard, and cloves. Place chops in large flat casserole, pour liquid over chops. Preheat oven to 375 degrees. Bake for 10 minutes. Be careful not to overcook, or chops may become tough. Before serving, use a toothpick to attach to each chop: a slice of orange, lemon, and top with cherry. Best served with boiled fluffy rice, and a dry white wine.

Serves 6.

Mildura, an Aboriginal word, means "red earth," which is certainly the color of the land surrounding this large town in the northwest part of the state of Victoria (the Southern tip of Australia). The area is renowned for its citrus orchards and vineyards. The use of fresh fruits, especially citrus and tropical fruits has become a distinctive part of Australia's cuisine.

To Australians, however, Mildura's main claim to fame is its Workingman's Club (built in 1938) which boasts the longest bar in the world. Pubs (hotels and bars) were prohibited in Mildura early this century, so private clubs were formed.

PRUNE STEAK

2 pounds choice steak
salt and pepper
2 tablespoons butter
1 large onion, sliced
1 cup flour
1 ¼ cups water
1 teaspoon soy sauce
2 tablespoons vinegar
¼ cup plum jam
½ pound prunes
2 tablespoons lemon rind
3 to 4 peeled tomatoes
chopped chives and parsley for garnish

- Slice steak into large squares, season with salt and pepper, pound with meat mallet. Melt butter and sauté onion in large pan until soft; remove and keep warm. In same pan, brown meat quickly on both sides; remove and keep warm. Sprinkle flour into pan, brown, blend in water. Stir in soy sauce, vinegar, and jam. Boil, stirring constantly, until mixture thickens. Return onions and meat to pan, add prunes and lemon rind. Cover and simmer gently for 30 to 40 minutes, until steak is tender. Arrange tomato wedges and heat through. Sprinkle with parsley and chives.

Serves 4 to 6.

If you are still not convinced that steak has a very definite place in the Australian menu, an observation made by the children's story writer, Beatrix Potter, will dispel any doubts: "The shearers evidently work very hard... and they live very well—-five meals a day, at three of which they have hot meat.... they get... 20 [shillings] a week, and rations—10 [pounds] of meat, 10 [pounds] of flour, 2 [pounds] sugar and 1 [pounds] tea per man per week."

—Beatrix Potter in *The Webbs' Australian Diary*, October 9, 1898.

AUSSIE BEEF RAGOUT

1 ½ pounds steak, cubed
¼ cup flour
3 to 4 slices lean bacon
4 tablespoons butter
1 cup peeled tomatoes
2 potatoes, peeled and sliced
2 onions, peeled and sliced
2 carrots, peeled and sliced
salt and pepper
½ cup claret
½ cup beef bouillon

- Roll steak cubes in flour. Cut bacon into large pieces and lightly fry in butter. Remove the bacon, then add meat and sauté until browned. Chop tomatoes into large pieces. Butter a casserole dish and place alternate layers of vegetables and meat. Combine claret and bouillon and pour over casserole. Bake, covered, for 2 ½ hours in a 375-degree oven. Boiled rice or lightly mashed potatoes are excellent companion dishes for this classic meal.

Serves 4.

ABOUT CLARET IN AUSTRALIA: Claret was probably the first of Australia's wines to receive truly popular Australian recognition (in contrast to international recognition, where Australia's wines of many types have done well in recent years.) For many years, the Australian beer-drinking tradition frowned upon the drinking of wine, a drink only imbibed by women and "pansies." Australia's clarets are light and dry, excellent for drinking as well as for cooking! One can almost always find an Australian claret in a large liquor store. If not, ask for a dry red wine. In the past ten years, Australia's wine making has come into its own, with corresponding enthusiastic consumption by

Australians. The wines are of all varieties, have excellent qualities, and are reasonably priced. (See the appendix for a few brief notes and recommendations on wines for visitors to Australia for the Olympic Games in Sydney in 2000.)

HAMBURGER HOT POT

There are many Australian recipes that derive from the English "hot pot" recipes. Here is a variation that uses hamburger meat, providing a recipe which is perhaps similar to American cooking.

4 tablespoons butter
1 pound ground beef
1 onion, chopped
2 cups canned tomatoes
salt and pepper
4 potatoes, peeled
¼ pound mozzarella cheese, sliced

- Melt butter and cook ground beef quickly over a high heat. Add onion, tomatoes, and salt and pepper to taste. Grease a casserole with margarine and put ½ of the hamburger mixture into casserole, then cover with half the sliced potato. Place another layer of meat mixture and cover with mozzarella cheese slices. Preheat the oven to 350 degrees and bake for 1 hour.

Serves 4.

BETSY'S PORCUPINES

1 ½ pounds ground beef
1 egg
1 small onion, chopped
½ cup uncooked rice
½ cup water
1 can (10 ounces) undiluted tomato soup

- Thoroughly mix meat, egg, and onion. Make into small balls and roll in rice. Place in casserole. Mix water and soup, pour over balls, and cook 1 hour. Make sure sauce covers balls while cooking.

Serves 4 to 6.

ABOUT PORCUPINES IN AUSTRALIA: Put simply, there are none. But what Australia does have is the echidna, a mammal or monotreme, which has stiff spikes or quills just like a porcupine. It is apparently unrelated to the rodent family which is the ancestor of the North American porcupine. The diet of the echidna is termites and other insects it can catch with its long sticky tongue.

Echidna

VEAL AND PINEAPPLE CASSEROLE

1 ½ pounds lean veal
4 ounces bacon (optional)
¼ teaspoon dried basil
¼ cup flour
1 tablespoon chopped parsley
2 onions, sliced
1 can (16 ounces) pineapple pieces (reserve liquid)
salt and pepper
½ cup beef bouillon
½ cup tomato juice

- Be sure to obtain the leanest veal you can. If bacon is used, make sure it also is as lean as possible. Mix basil with flour. Cut veal into about 1-inch pieces and roll in flour mixture. Place half in bottom of well-greased casserole and cover with half each of the bacon, parsley, onion, and pineapple pieces. Add salt and pepper to taste. Repeat layers until no more ingredients are left. Combine ¼ cup pineapple juice, bouillon, and tomato juice and pour over casserole. Bake, covered, for about 2 hours at 350 degrees. This dish goes best with boiled rice.

Serves 4 to 6.

ABOUT "TOMATO": Pronounced *too-mah-toe* by Australians. Oh! the inconsistencies of English pronunciation. If we say *too-mah-toe*, why don't we say *poo-tah-toe?* Instead, we say *pote-ate-oe*, just like Americans say *too-mate-oe*. Our bet is that a long time ago, Ben Franklin saw how silly these English inconsistencies were, and changed them in the name of efficiency!

SWEET AND SOUR LAMB

1 can (16 ounces) pineapple pieces
1 large onion, chopped
1 cup diced celery
1 medium green pepper, seeded and diced
4 tablespoons butter
1 ½ pounds cubed lamb*
2 tablespoons cornstarch
2 tablespoons soy sauce
2 tablespoons vinegar
¼ teaspoon pepper
1 teaspoon salt

- Drain pineapple pieces, reserving juice. Add water to juice to make 1 cup of liquid and set aside. Sauté drained pineapple, onion, celery, and pepper in 2 tablespoons butter until lightly browned. Remove from pan and set aside. Add remaining 2 tablespoons butter and cubed lamb to pan and cook until meat is brown on all sides.

- Blend together cornstarch, soy sauce, vinegar, salt, and pepper and stir in reserved pineapple liquid. Add to meat and cook, stirring until mixture boils and thickens. Cover and simmer for about 50 minutes, or until meat is tender. Add pineapple and remaining ingredients and cook another 15 minutes. Serve over freshly boiled rice.

Serves 4 to 6.

*ABOUT AUSTRALIAN LAMB: Lamb is probably the most widely preferred meat in Australia. To the visitor, Australian lamb has a strong, "gamy" aroma when cooking. After one has been in Australia some time, the nostrils adapt to this aroma, and one barely notices it at the many barbecues one attends. All countries have their own special and distinctive aromas. Australia's is one of sizzling lamb chops and beer yeast.

Some American supermarkets, once or twice a year, receive a shipment of New Zealand lamb, which is very similar to Australian lamb. If you plan to roast the lamb, you will not need to spice it with garlic and other herbs, because it already has a strong flavor.

SYDNEY BEEF SLICE

4 tablespoons tomato purée
¼ cup evaporated milk
¾ cup rolled oats
salt and pepper
1 egg
1 teaspoon dry mustard
1 onion, finely chopped
1 pound ground beef
4 servings instant potatoes
½ to 1 cup grated cheddar cheese

- Mix in bowl the purée, evaporated milk, oats, salt, pepper, egg, mustard, and onion. Using large fork and/or wooden spoon, thoroughly blend in the ground beef. Grease an 11 x 7-inch pan and spread mixture in base. Preheat oven to 375 degrees and bake for 30 minutes. Make up mashed potatoes according to packet directions and add half the grated cheese. Spoon over meat, then sprinkle rest of cheese on top. Bake another 20 minutes. Serve with a brown gravy and traditional vegetables that kids hate, such as broccoli or brussels sprouts. Kids love this with ketchup. Men eat it with a bottle of beer.

Serves 4.

SYDNEY is Australia's busiest city, epitomizing the contradictions of Australian culture. The futuristic opera house sparkles, poised over Sydney Harbor; the uncouth yahoos, larrikins, and drongoes swill beer on the hill at Sydney's Cricket Ground. In the year 2000, Sydney will host the Olympic Games. In the appendix, we have included a few small tips on restaurants and wines in Sydney. Be there!

*In the first edition of this book, we noted that small cans of beer were uncommon in Australia, and that beer was purchased by most Australians by the large bottle or large can (26 ounces, usually in cases of a dozen at a time). While these sizes of beer containers are still freely available in Australia, small cans and bottles similar in size to those in the U.S. are now the most commonly purchased beer items.

BEEF STEW BALLARAT*

3 slices bacon
2 pounds beef cubes
1 large carrot, sliced
1 medium onion, sliced
½ teaspoon salt
¼ teaspoon pepper
¼ cup flour
½ cup beef bouillon
1 cup claret
2 tablespoons tomato paste
1 clove garlic, crushed
½ teaspoon thyme
1 bay leaf
½ cup mushrooms

- Cut bacon into small squares and cook until crisp. Remove
  from pan and brown beef in bacon fat. Add sliced carrot,
  onion, salt, and pepper, then flour, stirring to coat meat. Add
  bouillon, claret, tomato paste, garlic, thyme, and bay leaves.
  Cover and simmer 2 hours. Cut mushrooms in quarters and
  sauté in butter. Add to stew. Serve stew with boiled whole
  potatoes topped with butter. Green peas are an excellent
  accompaniment. If you haven't finished all the claret while
  cooking, serve with the meal.
  Serves 6.

Cooking with wine and the old Australian tradition. Our
parents' generation never cooked dishes like this. In fact they
never cooked with wine at all. Cooking with wine became
popular with our generation, largely because Australian wines at
last began to break through the beer barrier. Up until around 25
years ago, one would be thought to be a "sissy" or a "plonko"
(skid row bum) if one bought wine in a pub. Beer was the drink,

and a true Australian drank nothing else. Gradually, Australia's red wines gained a measure of acceptance, especially her clarets, and now wine is consumed in large quantities, red and white.

Ballarat derives from the Aboriginal word "balaarat" meaning resting place, bend in the river. It is one of Australia's larger inland cities. It is chiefly known for its historical role in the gold rush years in the 1850s. The Ballarat gold fields yielded about $200 million, and one of the world's largest natural gold nuggets was found there—the *Welcome Nugget*.

IRISH STEW

1 pound chuck steak
salt and pepper
1 cup water
1 parsnip
1 carrot
½ pound onions
2 pounds potatoes
chopped parsley for garnish

- Trim fat from meat, cut into 1-inch squares. Place in pan with salt and pepper and cover with water. Peel parsnip, carrots, and onions and cut into slices, add to pan. Bring to boil and simmer for 30 minutes. Wash and peel potatoes, cut into large pieces, and place on top of stew. Sprinkle with salt (if preferred), place lid on, and simmer for 1 hour. Remove any excess fat and serve on plate with meat in center and potatoes all around. Sprinkle with chopped parsley when serving. This dish is excellent for cheap cuts of meat.

Serves 4 to 6.

ABOUT THE IRISH IN AUSTRALIA: Our parents may not have cooked with wine, but they did cook Irish Stew. It is well known that Australia was first settled by convicts. Many of these convicts were Irish (the Irish were convicted at a much higher rate than other social groups in England in the eighteenth century). Australians can therefore claim, with some degree of emotional commitment, Irish stew to be an important part of their heritage.

Furthermore, it was an Irishman, Lalor, who led Australia's only violent revolt at the Eureka Stockade, near Ballarat in 1854. He was also assisted in this revolt by an American, James McGill. The gold miners demonstrated against excessive mining license fees, police brutality, and many other matters that made life on the gold fields a severe hardship. About 1,000 miners barricaded themselves in the stockade on December 1, 1854. They were charged by 187 government troops (11 mounted on horseback). 30 miners and 5 soldiers were killed. The government changed its policies. Australians consider this event to have been the nation's birth of democracy.

LAMB LEFTOVERS

In America there are many recipes for leftover chicken and turkey, because these are very popular everyday foods. In Australia, the everyday popular food is lamb, so what to do with lamb leftovers? Be careful not to overcook this dish, or the lamb will have that "cooked twice" taste.

1 green pepper
1 pound cooked lamb, minced
1 onion, chopped
1 to 2 cups dry stuffing mix
1 egg
1 teaspoon Worcestershire sauce
6 slices lean bacon

- Place green pepper in cold water and bring to boil. Let stand for 3 minutes, then core and finely chop. Combine lamb, pepper, onion, and stuffing mix, then bind with egg and Worcestershire. Form into round patty shapes about 1 inch thick. Wrap bacon around edges of patties, secure with toothpicks. Place on cookie tray. Heat in 350-degree oven until bacon is crisp and onion browned.
Serves 4 to 6.

ABOUT LEFTOVERS IN AUSTRALIA: Leftovers are the food that a sundowner would be offered. A sundowner was a vagabond in the late nineteenth century who constantly walked from one settlement to another, just arriving at a homestead at sundown—in time to eat, but not in time to do chores. There were many sundowners during the 1930s during the Great Depression. More colorful were the *Swaggies* who "humped their bluey" (carried their belongings rolled up in a blanket with a billy [bush kettle, see page 259] hanging from its side), from homestead to homestead asking to work in exchange for a good meal. The sense of mateship and freedom these nomadic men had, has been

119

recorded in many bush ballads. The most famous of these is "Waltzing Matilda" in which a swagman commits suicide rather than lose his freedom:

And his ghost may be heard as you pass by that billabong
"You'll come a waltzing Matilda with me!"
—"Waltzing Matilda," A.B. ("Banjo") Paterson, about 1905
Billabong is the aboriginal word for a small pond.

SEA PIE

This special brown stew has a delicious upper crust topping with a scone-like consistency.

Upper crust:
1 cup flour
1 pinch salt
½ teaspoon baking powder
½ cup shortening
water

Stew:
1 pound beef cubes
salt and pepper
3 onions
6 potatoes

- Sift flour, salt, and baking powder. Rub shortening into flour until mixture looks like bread crumbs. Mix slowly with water to make a very stiff paste, then knead lightly. Cover while you make the stew.

- Sprinkle beef cubes with salt and pepper, place in pan with just enough boiling water to cover. Simmer for 30 minutes. Peel onions and potatoes and cut into small pieces. Add to meat. Roll upper crust dough into a round a little less than the top of the pan. Lay it on the meat, replace pan lid, and cook for an additional 1 ½ hours. When cooked, cut the upper crust in four pieces and place on a warm plate. Arrange the stew on a hot platter and place the crust on top.
  Serves 6.

Why is it called Sea Pie? This tasty stew was designed to be cooked at sea, most likely in the sea-faring times when many convicts were transported on ships from England to Australia. Sailing ships of those times did not have ovens, which means that one could not cook a real pie because a real pie requires pastry to be cooked in an oven. Sea Pie gets around this problem by producing a "crust" that is cooked in the pan.

GREEK PISTACHIO

2 pounds lean ground beef
1 chopped onion
2 cloves mashed garlic
2 tablespoons butter
1 pound spaghetti

White sauce:
6 tablespoons flour
4 tablespoons butter
1 cup milk
1 beaten egg
4 ounces grated Parmesan cheese

- Simmer minced steak, onion, and garlic in melted butter for 20 minutes. Cook spaghetti in salted water until *al dente*, about 5 minutes, then drain. Grease a large meat dish or casserole. Put in a layer of spaghetti. Cover with a layer of meat and sprinkle with grated cheese. Continue in this manner until all spaghetti and meat is used.

- To make sauce: melt butter, stir in flour, and cook on low heat for one minute. Stir in milk and cook until smooth, then add in beaten egg and cheese.

- Cover the spaghetti and meat with the white sauce and sprinkle with grated cheese. Bake at 325 degrees for 30 minutes. This recipe has been in our family recipe books for four generations. This is unusual, considering our English background. The white sauce with the eggs added, forms a lovely soufflé-type topping on this casserole.

Serves 8 to 10.

SPAGHETTI CASSEROLE

4 tablespoons butter
1 clove garlic, crushed
1 cup chopped onion
1 ½ pounds ground beef
1 pound ripe tomatoes, skinned, *or* 1 can (16 ounces)
    whole tomatoes
1 cup water
1 teaspoon Worcestershire sauce
salt and pepper
1 pinch oregano
1 pound spaghetti
1 cup grated sharp cheese
parsley for garnish

- Sauté garlic and onion in butter until transparent. Add ground beef and brown well. Add fresh or canned tomatoes with juice to meat mixture with water (bouillon if preferred), Worcestershire, salt, pepper, and oregano. Cover and simmer about 15 minutes.

- Cook spaghetti in boiling water for 8 minutes, or until tender but firm. Drain and turn into greased casserole dish. Top with meat mixture, dot with butter and sprinkle with grated cheese. Bake in 350-degree oven until cheese is melted and brown, about 15 minutes. Garnish with parsley when serving.

Serves 6 to 8.

WALNUT CURRY

1 ½ pounds beef cubes
4 tablespoons butter
½ cup chopped onion
2 teaspoons curry powder
1 banana, sliced
1 medium tomato, peeled and diced
½ cup chopped walnuts
2 cups bouillon
1 teaspoon salt

- Brown meat in butter and remove from pan. Sauté onion and curry powder for 3 minutes; add banana, tomato, walnuts, and beef. Cover with bouillon, add salt, and simmer for 1 to 1 ½ hours. When cooked, pour into large warmed tourine, decorate with walnut halves. Serve with fluffy boiled rice.

Serves 4 to 6.

OLD ASIAN AUSSIE COOKING: The Asian influence on Australian cooking dates back WELL to the beginning of the twentieth century:

His cook was a Cantonese-Asian at least!
Who thought enough curry as good as a feast;
And his ex-soldier, from Antrim, named Barney,
Used to rouse the black stockmen in bad Hindustani.
—"Chillianwallah Station," by John Manifold, 1940s

CURRIED SPAGHETTI

4 ounces thin spaghetti
4 tablespoons butter
1 cup chopped onion
1 ½ teaspoons curry powder
1 pound ground beef
2 medium tomatoes, peeled and diced
2 tablespoons dried mushrooms
1 cup tomato purée
1 cup beef bouillon

- Cook spaghetti in plenty of water for 8 minutes. Drain. Sauté onion and curry powder in butter until onion is transparent. Add meat and cook 5 minutes. Add tomatoes, dried mushrooms, tomato purée, and bouillon. Grease casserole and preheat oven to 375 degrees. Place small amount of mixture in base of casserole, empty spaghetti on top, then cover with rest of mixture. Cover and bake 20 minutes.

Serves 4 to 6.

CURRIED SPAGHETTI: Boil it and then bake it! Older Aussies have eaten canned spaghetti for many years—even cold in sandwiches (see Sandwiches and Scones, Chapter 3). One thing is for sure: this recipe predates the influx of Italian immigrants to Australia in the twentieth century, and certainly owes little of its origin to India!

QUEENSLAND CURRY

This recipe is a great favorite. Admittedly, one cannot argue that curries are Australian—naturally they are Indian. But our Indian friends tell us that curries with fruit such as this dish are rare in India, probably nonexistent. There are relatively few Indians in Australia, but many Indian settlements throughout the Pacific Islands, with which Australia has had close contact.

4 tablespoons butter
2 onions, chopped
1 banana, sliced
1 green apple, chopped
2 tomatoes, skinned and chopped
1 tablespoon curry powder
1 ½ pounds beef cubes
1 cup canned pineapple pieces, reserve juice
¼ cup flour
salt and pepper
½ cup coconut
4 tablespoons golden raisins
2 tablespoons lemon juice

- Melt butter in a saucepan, and sauté onions, banana, apple, tomatoes, and curry powder. Add meat and brown. Remove pineapple from can and add water to the remaining juice to make 1¼ cups. Add flour and cook 2 minutes, then add pineapple liquid, salt, and pepper. Bring to boil and simmer 1½ hours. Add pineapple pieces, coconut, raisins, and lemon juice. Simmer an additional 20 to 30 minutes. Check often for consistency, add liquid if necessary. Serve on bed of boiled rice. Make available an array of nuts (almonds and cashews), carrot sticks, coconut, celery sticks, and apple slices to be eaten on the side.

Serves 4 to 6.

YOGURT CURRY

2 tablespoons butter
2 onions, sliced
1 small clove garlic
1 ½ pounds beef cubes
½ teaspoon marsala
1 tablespoon curry powder
1 teaspoon tumeric
salt
1 ¼ cups beef bouillon
1 ¼ cups plain yogurt

- Sauté onions and garlic in butter until transparent. Add beef and continue to cook until meat changes color. Now add marsala, curry powder, and turmeric, and sauté 5 minutes. Add salt and bouillon, cover, and simmer about 2 hours or until meat is tender. Finally, add yogurt, stir well and simmer with lid off until most liquid has evaporated. Serve on bed of boiled long-grain rice. Provide small dishes of chopped tomato, chopped onions, banana slices, coconut, and pineapple pieces.

Serves 4 to 6.

POTATO CURRY

4 tablespoons oil
2 onions, sliced
clove garlic
4 large potatoes, peeled and diced (not too small)
1 cup water
1 can (16 ounces) tomatoes, drained (reserve liquid)
1 ½ tablespoons coconut milk
½ teaspoon *each*, ground tumeric, cinnamon, cardamom, black
pepper, cumin, ginger, sugar, chili powder, and salt.

- Heat oil, add onion and fry until transparent. Add garlic and
  potatoes and fry 2 minutes more. Add remaining ingredients, bring to boil, and simmer until potatoes are cooked.
  Add reserved tomato liquid if needed. Serve with boiled rice.
  Delicious vegetarian meal or can be a vegetable dish with a
  plain grill.

Serves 4.

VARIATION: Serve with the following accompaniments for a
vegetarian meal:

Natural yogurt with diced cucumber and mint
Bananas sliced in lemon juice
Pappadums
Mango and Port chutney (See page 130)
Pineapple pieces

PAPPADUMS are plain or spiced wafer thin brittle disks made
from dal paste, that swell into tasty crispbreads when pan fried,
toasted, or microwaved.

MANGO AND PORT CHUTNEY

4 medium mangoes, chopped
¾ cup port
1 cup chopped raisins
2 teaspoons grated fresh ginger
2 small fresh red chilies, finely chopped
2 cups sugar
3 cups brown sugar
2 teaspoons yellow mustard seeds

- Combine mangoes in large pan with all ingredients. Stir constantly over heat without boiling until sugar is dissolved. Bring to boil, reduce heat. Simmer, uncovered, for 1 ½ hours or until chutney is thick. Towards end of cooking time, watch carefully, and stir occasionally. Pour into hot, sterilized jars. Seal when cold.

Makes 3 cups.

ABOUT MANGOES: These are a succulent tropical fruit widely available in Australia and the United States. Truly fresh mangoes will give off a delightful perfume if left sitting in one's kitchen. Don't leave them sitting too long, though, or they will become overripe. These fruits are very popular in the northeastern part of Australia (the tropical area) as we see from the following poem:

mangoes are not cigarettes
mangoes are fleshy skinful passion fruits
mangoes are hungry to be sucked
mangoes are glad to be stuck in the teeth
mangoes like slush and kissing
—"Mangoes," Richard Tipping

ABOUT PORT IN AUSTRALIA: Apart from beer and wine, Australians also drink quite a lot of port. It is probably more popular as an after dinner drink than are cordials (liqueurs). One good reason for this popularity is the wide availability of excellent Australian ports, rich in flavor and light in body. These ports are also excellent taken after dinner with cheese and crackers, another popular Aussie practice.

HONEY SWEET POTATOES

2 pounds sweet potatoes
4 tablespoons butter
1 cup pecans, chopped
1 teaspoon grated orange rind
1 cup orange juice
¼ cup honey
cinnamon
chopped chives

- Peel potatoes and chop into large cubes. Bring water to boil, add potatoes and cook, uncovered, until just tender. Drain potatoes into a colander and set aside. Melt butter in the pan, add pecans, and cook until lightly browned. Remove pecans and drain on kitchen paper. To butter in pan, add orange rind, orange juice, honey and cinnamon to taste. Bring to a boil and reduce liquid to half. Add potatoes to liquid and heat through, stirring gently. Sprinkle nuts and chives over the potatoes just before serving. Use the orange-colored sweet potato. Kamaruka is best.
Serves 6.

Chapter 7

Salads

*I*t is not so much the conglomeration of different vegetables that makes the Australian salad so "typical" but
rather the way the salad is served. This reflects a general difference in table manners between Australians and Americans. At
our first Thanksgiving dinner many years ago, which we were
invited to by some very kind Americans who saw that we
were lonely, we were fascinated to discover that all the wonderful food dishes were placed on the dining table, and passed
around for each person to choose. The Australian tradition is
quite different. All diners' plates are kept in the kitchen, where
the food is divided among the plates. These are then brought
into the dining room and placed before the guests, just as in a
restaurant.

The American practice of beginning meals with a salad is
virtually unknown in Australia. The salad is usually eaten as a
meal in itself, as described here, or kept to the side and eaten
along with the main meal. Our older rellies (relatives), when they
visit, are annoyed by this American practice. They keep their
small dish of salad, then empty it onto the main dish when it's
served!

If you would prefer less formality (which is more Australian,
actually) you might like to pack up your salad plates and head
for the beach. In this case, choose your largest cooler (called a car

fridge or "Esky" in Australia), carefully lay out the salad on separate disposable plates (strong ones so they won't absorb too much moisture and bend in two when you lift them out), cover with plastic wrap, and place in your cooler along with a plentiful supply of cold beer for the men (!) and soft drinks (soda) for the kids, and separately, a couple of thermos flasks of tea (for everyone). (Tea kept this way doesn't taste right unless prepared properly: see cuppa tea, page 225) A few sandwiches and slices of plain bread and butter will also go down well. Then fill a container with a selection of cookies.

Now you're ready for a day on the beach. Load the boot of your car (*trunk* to Americans) with a cricket bat and ball, a large sun hat, and you're in for a relaxing, sun-drenched day in the healthy salt air. Ah! the fine white and beige sand sifting through the toes... the gently swaying grass on the dunes... the sheer red cliffs facing the sea....

A day can pass by very easily swimming in the crystal water of Australia's surf beaches, and playing cricket (see pages 221-22) on the sand. These activities do wonders for the appetite—you need to have a *big* cooler. Australia is blessed with thousands of miles of sandy beaches, only a tiny portion of them "developed" in the sense that they are patrolled, have car parks, and so on. Laws will not allow individuals to own or build up to the ocean shoreline. Australians who travel abroad—whether to Europe or the United States — are aghast that one would either have to pay to get on to a beach, or that individuals could actually own land and houses right down to the water. The drive down Big Sur in California, while stunning in its own right, seems defaced to an Australian because of the houses right down to the shoreline.

If you would like to serve your Australian salad in surroundings without sand but retaining the Aussie style, be sure to set your table with a "bread and butter plate" for each guest. Just about every Australian meal is served with bread and butter, Australian salads especially. The Australian bread and butter plate is about the size of a small plate that Americans would use for salad.

AUSTRALIAN SALAD

thinly sliced firm tomatoes
short celery sticks
grated carrot
thinly sliced cucumber
beet root
thinly sliced orange
thin slices of banana
one or two pieces of apple
fresh pineapple squares
fresh whole lettuce leaves
parsley
grated cheese
cold cooked peas
cold cooked string beans
small boiled baby potatoes (cold with butter)
sliced boiled egg
gherkins
pickled onions
canned salmon
raisins
avocado
potted steak (see page 38)

- Use as wide a variety of fresh garden vegetables as you can
  find. The Australian salad is most often served with a few
  thin slices of cold cuts, such as roast beef, ham, German
  sausage, chicken, or a little potted meat. Naturally, these cold
  dishes are most popular in summertime, especially to clean
  up any leftover turkey from Christmas dinner. The cold cuts
  are usually arranged flat on one side of the plate, nestling
  against various ingredients, with crisp lettuce on the outside
  of the plate. Thin slices of orange, split and twisted are
  common—intended to be eaten as well as for decoration.

VICTORIA SALAD

6 medium tomatoes
salt, pepper, and sugar
1 cup grated cheddar cheese
1 tablespoon finely chopped pineapple
1 tablespoon finely chopped nuts
1 cup finely chopped lettuce
1 teaspoon finely chopped parsley
1 teaspoon chopped scallions
cayenne pepper
mayonnaise
lettuce leaf to serve on

- Cut off tops of tomatoes and scoop out centers, sprinkle with salt, pepper, and sugar to taste. Mash the tomato pulp well and mix in cheese, pineapple, and nuts, lettuce, parsley, and scallions. Fill tomato shells with mixture, sprinkle top with cayenne pepper. Top with a small daub of thick mayonnaise. Set each tomato on a crisp lettuce leaf. Serve chilled. Don't forget the bread and butter.

Serves 4 to 6.

GOLDEN SALAD

8 ounces cheddar cheese
4 medium firm tomatoes
6 radishes
1 head lettuce
1 can (14 ounces) pineapple rings
French or Italian dressing
mint leaves for garnish

• Cut the cheese into small cubes, the tomatoes into wedges, and radishes into roses. Tear lettuce into pieces and place in salad bowl. Arrange pineapple rings in circle, tomato wedges around edge. Place cheese cubes in center, radish rose in each pineapple ring. Garnish with a few mint leaves. Add dressing to taste.

Serves 4 to 6

COCONUT SALAD

2 peeled and chopped oranges
1 can (8 ounces) crushed pineapple
3 ounces shredded coconut
⅓ cup sour cream

• Combine oranges and drained pineapple in a clear salad bowl. Add shredded coconut and sour cream. Mix all ingredients, decorate with a curled slice of orange or finely shredded orange peel. Serve immediately.

Serves 4 to 6.

JOAN'S PACIFIC SALAD

fluffy boiled rice
grated carrot
pineapple bits and some juice
currants
golden raisins
chopped tops of scallions
cooked peas
chopped nuts (optional)
coconut (optional)

- Mix all ingredients, varying amounts according to taste. Serve on large shallow dish, surrounded by orange and lemon slices. This salad is an especially good companion to sweet and sour dishes, casseroles with pineapple, and curries.

ABOUT THE PACIFIC: The influence of the Pacific Islands on Australian food has been gradual, but sure. The use of pineapple in many recipes is no doubt a product of Australia's proximity to the Pacific Islands and the fruit's abundance in northeastern Australia. We have eaten salads similar to this in Hawaii, although in the Pacific Islands the use of raisins and currants is less common.

GREEN AND GOLD SALAD

Lettuce leaves
1 cucumber, thinly sliced
1 can (11 ounces) mandarin segments, well drained and sliced
3 bananas, sliced
2 pears, sliced
2 avocados, sliced

Chutney dressing:
½ cup mayonnaise
½ cup sour cream
4 tablespoons chutney
¼ teaspoon curry powder
Dash of Tabasco
4 tablespoons oil
2 tablespoons white wine vinegar
Pinch of salt

* Arrange lettuce leaves in large salad bowl, and place fruit and vegetables in a pattern of green and gold. Mix chutney dressing and serve in small dish placed in center of bowl. Best prepared as close to eating time as possible.

ABOUT GREEN AND GOLD: Green and gold are Australia's national colors in international sporting events. The gold represents the wattle (see glossary) and green is for the leaves of the eucalyptus trees.

QUEENSLAND SALAD

2 bacon slices, chopped
2 avocados, peeled and sliced
2 mangoes, peeled and sliced
⅓ cup chopped nuts (pecans or walnuts)
1 head lettuce (mignonette, radicchio, etc.)

Dressing:
¼ cup olive oil
4 tablespoons lemon juice
2 tablespoons heavy cream
1 teaspoon mild mustard

- Cook chopped bacon in a pan until crisp. Drain on kitchen paper. Arrange avocado, mango, nuts, and bacon over a bed of lettuce. Combine all dressing ingredients in a jar and shake well. Top salad with dressing. Make close to eating time.

Serves 4 to 6.

SUNSHINE SALAD

1 can (8 ounces) crushed pineapple
4 tablespoons vinegar
½ teaspoon mustard
1 package (3 ounces) lemon Jell-O
1 cup grated carrot
½ cup chopped celery

* Drain the pineapple. Reserve syrup and to it add vinegar, mustard, and enough water to make 2 cups liquid. Dissolve Jell-O in the liquid, allow to cool, then add pineapple, carrot, and celery. Pour into a flat glass dish and set in the fridge until it sets—about 2 hours. Cut into squares for ease of serving.

Serves 4.

CAULIFLOWER AND BEET-ROOT SALAD

1 small cauliflower
2 small fresh beets
¼ pound cheese, your choice
2 eggs

Dressing:
1 egg yolk
2 tablespoons oil
2 tablespoons heavy cream
1 teaspoon vinegar
pinch of salt and pepper

- Boil the cauliflower and beet-root separately, until tender. Leave till cold. Divide cauliflower into small sprigs, and cut beets into thin strips. Cut cheese into small cubes. Hard boil eggs. Chop the white and rub yolk through a sieve. Make a border of cauliflower on a dish. Fill center with beet-root strips mixed with cheese and chopped egg white. Make the dressing: stir yolk vigorously while adding oil, drop by drop. Then stir in cream, and gradually add vinegar and salt and pepper. Pour the dressing over salad and sprinkle with egg yolk.

Serves 4 to 6.

Chapter 8

Cookies and Slices

*C*ookies and tasty slices (slabs of cake or dessert, cut into 2" squares) are made for all occasions in Australia; for entertaining, and to have around for the kids to stave off their constant hunger.

Australians have a casual lifestyle, and an enviable openness in their social life. A typical way to spend the weekend is to "drop in" on friends and rellies (relatives). This means what it says. One may be visited by people without warning. Many Australian households keep a constant supply of cookies and slices that can be produced, along with a cup of tea, for unexpected guests. An easy solution to this pleasant, but demanding custom, would be to serve store-bought cookies. However, as the English say, this simply would not do. The cookies and slices are often the focus of conversation, and it may be at this time that new recipes are exchanged and discussed.

Cookies are most often served in the morning at "morning tea" (around 10:30 a.m.) at which time everything stops. Most places of work sound a whistle or bell (we have seen this in factories, schools, universities, and government departments) when it is time to break for tea.

ANZAC BISCUITS (COOKIES)

My mother used to make these chewy mouth-watering cookies every few weeks, not only on ANZAC day.* One dreams of their treacle flavor.

½ cup (1 stick) butter
1 teaspoon treacle (molasses)
1 teaspoon baking soda
¾ cup fine sugar
2 tablespoons boiling water
¾ cup flaked coconut
1 cup oatmeal
¾ cup flour

- In saucepan place butter, treacle, baking soda, and sugar, and mix with boiling water. Bring slowly to boil, remove and add coconut, oatmeal, and flour, mixing well. Place large spoonfuls of mixture about 3 inches apart on well greased cookie tray. Bake in 275-degree oven for 25 minutes.

Makes 2 dozen.

ABOUT AUSSIE COOKIES: Not many Australians use the word "cookie." All cookies are "biscuits" to Australians. And what Americans call "biscuits" Australians call "scones" (see scones, page 44). Generally speaking, Australian cookies are drier and less chewy than American cookies. ANZAC biscuits are an exception.

ABOUT ANZAC DAY: ANZAC Day is celebrated in Australia on April 25. On this day in 1915, the ANZACs (Australian and New Zealand Army Corps) landed at Gallipoli, and suffered the worst defeat in Australian military history. The fallen soldiers of all wars are now commemorated on ANZAC Day. ANZAC biscuits, because they were soft, were thought to keep better when shipped to Australia's troops during World War I. Thus, they came to be called ANZACs.

AFGHANS

In the Australian holiday season, (Christmas through New Year) moms everywhere make these chocolate cookies. In a time when the abundance of chocolate can cause chocolate cookie blues, Afghan biscuits provide a distinctive chocolate taste that simply does not exist anywhere else.

¾ cup butter
⅓ cup fine sugar
3-6 drops vanilla
1 pinch salt
⅓ cup plain flour
¾ cup self-rising flour
2 tablespoons cocoa
½ cup cornflakes

- Cream butter and sugar, add salt and vanilla to taste. Sift dry flours and cocoa and add to mixture, mixing well. Add cornflakes and mix thoroughly. Place on cold greased cookie tray, and bake 15 minutes at 375 degrees. These cookies are great plain, but even better topped with just a dollop of chocolate frosting (see chocolate icing, page 215).

Makes 1 dozen.

WHY ARE THEY CALLED AFGHANS? This is a very old recipe. We have no idea how these cookies got their name. They are a dark brown, however, and it's possible that someone in the outback who came across an Afghan and his camel, thought the cookies were the color of the Afghan (or maybe his camel). Yes, there are camels in the Australian outback. They were introduced in 1840.

ABOUT "MOM" AND "MUM" "Mom" is spelled "Mum" in Australian, and it can have other meanings as well as one's mother. If you are asked to "keep mum" don't tell anyone — it means to keep a secret. The pronunciation of "mum" and "mummy" is also different from the "mommy" or drawn out vowel in "mammy." Aussie kids say "mummy" or "mum" using the short sound of "u" as in "hug."

CHRISTMAS COOKIES

At Christmastime, Aussies always do their "Christmas baking" and prepare a variety of tasty morsels that are even more succulent than the usual fare provided at afternoon teas. Here are a few of the best, starting with our favorite, mainly because of the rum!

RUM FUDGE BALLS

1 can (14 ounces) condensed milk
½ cup coconut
2 tablespoons cocoa
1 cup plain cookies (crushed)
1 teaspoon vanilla
2 tablespoons rum
coconut for rolling

- Use the plainest cookies you can. If you can find cookies sometimes called "English tea" these will be fine. Mix all ingredients (except reserved coconut for rolling) thoroughly together, and roll into balls. Cover with coconut, chill in refrigerator. Beer drinkers have been known to sneak these while no one was looking.

VARIATION: Take slivers of dates and encase them in the above mixture. Roll in chocolate sprinkles, chill.
Makes 2 dozen.

CHOCOLATE BALLS

4 tablespoons butter
¾ cup condensed milk
3 tablespoons cocoa
¼ cup coconut
1 package (16 ounces) plain cookies
1 package (10 ounces) marshmallows

* Use the plainest cookies you can find. Melt butter and heat milk very slowly. Add cocoa and coconut. Let it sit 5 minutes while you crush the cookies. Add cookies to mixture, mix thoroughly. Roll into small balls, chill.

Makes 2 dozen.

APRICOT COCONUT BALLS

2 cups dried apricots
1 can (14 ounces) condensed milk
1 cup cornflakes
1 cup coconut

* Finely crush the cornflakes. Mince apricots and add milk and cornflakes. Roll into balls, cover with coconut, chill.

Makes 2 dozen.

COCONUT RUFFS

1 can (14 ounces) condensed milk
½ pound (3 ½ cups) coconut
1 teaspoon vanilla
2 tablespoons cocoa

- Thoroughly mix together all ingredients. Place teaspoonfuls on cold cookie tray and bake in 375-degree oven for 10 minutes. Keep refrigerated.

Makes 2 dozen.

TUTTY FRUITY

1 can (14 ounces) evaporated milk
1 passion fruit
Juice of ½ lemon
1 banana
Juice of 1 orange
¾ cup sugar

- Combine all ingredients, beat thoroughly and pour into flat pan, chill. Cut into small squares for serving.
Makes 12 squares.

ABOUT CHRISTMAS IN AUSTRALIA: When we were a kids, just about all our Christmas cards showed scenes of snow-covered villages or families sitting around cozy fires by their Christmas trees. Hardly any Australians have seen snow, and Christmas comes right at the beginning of summer. Australia is still part of the British Commonwealth, but Aussies no longer apologize for their English heritage. Instead they have Christmas dinner on the beach, and send Christmas cards with Australian scenes of flora and fauna. But where cooking traditions are concerned, they still produce these wonderful Christmas cookies which most likely have English roots. The tie with England is difficult to sever.

MINCE TARTS

These and many other types of cookies and slices are very popular in Australia around Christmastime, and are not often served during the rest of the year. Here is one of those recipes which happens to be Dad's favorite.

Fruit mince:
¾ cup chopped raisins
6 tablespoons brown sugar
¼ cup chopped glacé fruits
2 tablespoons brandy
½ teaspoon allspice
rind of ½ lemon
1 grated apple
3 ounces currants
¼ cup mixed peel
¼ cup shortening
rind of ½ orange

Tart pastry
1 pastry (see Amy Johnson Cake, page 168)
egg yolk for glazing
confectioners' sugar

- Mix all fruit mince ingredients thoroughly. Use the juice of lemon, orange, or sherry or brandy if mixture is too dry.
- Roll out the pastry to about 1 inch thick. Cut into 2 different size rounds: the bottoms will be slightly larger than the tops. Line muffin tins with pastry, spoon in fruit mince. Wet edges of pastry cases, place on tops, and pinch together with fingers. Glaze with egg yolk. Bake in 450-degree oven for about 10 minutes. Cool on wire rack and dust with sugar.
Makes 12 tarts.

MARSHMALLOW SLICE

6 cups cornflakes
1 cup coconut
1 cup flour
¾ cup brown sugar
1 pinch salt
1 pound (4 sticks) butter, melted

• Mix dry ingredients, add melted butter, mix thoroughly. Press with fingers into 10-inch square pan. Bake in 350-degree oven for 15 minutes. Allow to cool. Make glaze.

Glaze:
1 cup sugar
¾ cup water
1 to 4 drops vanilla
1 tablespoon gelatin (dissolved in hot water)

1 cup chocolate chips, melted

• Boil together sugar, water, and vanilla. Add gelatin, mix thoroughly, allow to cool. Whip until mixture becomes fluffy. Spread on cooled cookie mixture and top with melted chocolate. Cut into 2" squares.
Makes 10 squares.

ABOUT CHRISTMAS EATING: It happens everywhere—overeating on special occasions. It happens in Australia too:

Stuffed with pudding to his gizzard
Uncle James lets out a snore,
Auntie Flo sprawls like a lizard
On the back verandah floor.
In the scrub the cows are drowsing,
Dogs are dreaming in the shade.

Fat and white, the mare is browsing,
Cropping softly, blade by blade.
It is hot. Mosquitoes whirring
Uncle James rubs his knee:
"Flo," he whispers, "are you stirring?
It's near time to get the tea."
—"Bush Christmas," by David Martin, 1940s

VANILLA SLICES

Vanilla slices are a perennial favorite. The center is a type of thick vanilla custard. We have found something similar to slices in American bakeries, but the cream filling is not the same consistency, and as usual, there's too much of it.

1 recipe flaky pastry (see Amy Johnston Cake, page 168)
1 tablespoon cornstarch
¾ cup milk
1 tablespoon sugar
1 teaspoon vanilla
1 egg
Vanilla icing (page 214)

- Roll out pastry into 2 thin strips of equal size, about 1/8 inch thick. Prick all over with fork and bake until crisp and golden in 400-degree oven for about 15 to 20 minutes. Blend cornstarch with milk and sugar, stir continuously over low heat until boiled and thick. Remove, stir in vanilla and beaten egg. Spread between the 2 strips of pastry (you should have about ½ inch of cream between the two layers of pastry) and frost top with vanilla icing. Cool in refrigerator, cut into 1 ½-inch squares.

Makes 10 two-inch squares.

ABOUT EATING VANILLA SLICES: These slices are hard to eat with composure, especially in Australia where it's not all that common at afternoon tea to be supplied with a dessert fork or spoon with which to eat these pieces of succulence. (Of course, one would receive the proper culinary implements if vanilla slices were served as a dessert at dinner, but this would be unusual). The problem is that when you bite them, the delicious cream filling oozes out the sides, making it difficult to manage one's teacup, saucer, and plate and catch the dripping cream at the same time. Kids have no problem: they lick around all four sides first.

YO YO BISCUITS (COOKIES)

An Australian expatriate dreams of these addictive little cookies at least once a week. Our rellies (relatives) make these all the time, about as much as American moms bake chocolate chip cookies or brownies. These are the blue chip of cookies. Once you have tasted them, you won't rest until you have devoured them all.

¾ cup (1 ½ sticks) butter
½ cup fine sugar
¾ cup flour
2 ounces custard powder*
Vanilla icing (page 214)

- Cream butter and sugar. Sift flour and custard powder 3 times. Mix into butter and sugar and work until a stiff dough is obtained. Roll into small balls about the size of large marbles, or a little bigger. If in doubt, it's best to be on the small side, as these cookies will be joined together with frosting. Place each ball on a greased cookie sheet, pressing down on the top of each with the back of a fork. Bake at 350 degrees for 15 to 20 minutes. When cool, join together in pairs with vanilla icing. They look like yo-yo's! And they taste like nothing you have ever tasted before.

Makes 12 yo-yos.

*ABOUT CUSTARD POWDER. Custard powder is a mainstay of every Australian kitchen. Hopefully your gourmet food store will stock this very useful product, made in England as well as Australia. Custard is easily made from this powder. In this recipe, custard powder gives the cookies their distinctive, smooth taste. Custard powder and other Australian specialty items may be purchased from Aussie mail-order companies listed in the appendix.

MELTING MOMENTS

These tasty morsels are nearly the same as Yo-Yos but contain cornstarch instead of custard powder, so they are fine for people with egg allergies.

¾ cup (1 ½ sticks) butter
½ cup castor sugar
¾ cup plain flour
½ cup cornstarch

- Cream butter and sugar, fold in sifted flour and cornstarch. Place by teaspoonfuls on a baking tray and bake in a 325-degree oven for 15 minutes. Do not join with icing, as in Yo-Yos, because these morsels are already sugary enough!
Makes 1 dozen.

WALNUT DELIGHTS

Pastry:
10 tablespoons butter
1 cup self-rising flour
1 tablespoon fine sugar
1 pinch salt
1 egg yolk
1 tablespoon water

- Rub butter into flour, add sugar, and salt. Mix to a stiff dough with egg yolk beaten with a little water. Roll out thin and line 8 greased muffin tins.

Filling:
4 tablespoons butter
⅓ cup fine sugar
1 egg
½ cup finely chopped walnuts

- Cream butter and sugar, then add eggs and walnuts. Pour into pastry in muffin cups. Bake in a 325-degree oven for 15 minutes.

Makes 8.

ABOUT WALNUTS IN AUSTRALIA: Yes, it's true. There are no walnuts indigenous to Australia. They were imported into Australia by our English ancestors along with rabbits and other vermin. Fortunately, walnuts were one of the good things they brought. You could substitute pecans for walnuts if you prefer, although the result will be a slightly less zesty taste. In olden days, pecans were not often used in Australian cooking. They are used more and more today. We have introduced pecan pie to many Aussie friends and rellies, and it has proved to be a most popular item.

ANNE'S CHERRY RIPE

Cherry Ripes are one of the commercial candy bars that Aussie expatriates dream about, and which are unavailable in the United States. Here is a homemade version from one of our rellies.

½ pound plain cookies, crushed
6 tablespoons shortening
1 tablespoon fine sugar
¾ cup evaporated milk
½ teaspoon red food coloring
½ teaspoon almond extract
¼ cup glazed cherries
1 cup coconut
chocolate icing (see page 215)

- Grease a 7 x 11-inch shallow baking pan, and arrange a layer of cookies in base. Melt shortening and mix in remaining ingredients, blending thoroughly. Spread over cookies and allow to stand for about 1 hour. Place in freezer, remove when frozen and cover with thick layer of chocolate icing. When thawed, cut into 1 ½-inch squares.

Makes 24 squares.

ABOUT CANDY BARS: There are a number of candy bars that are dear to the heart of every Aussie. We have tried, at times to reproduce them in the U.S., but with poor results. The two we adore most used to be made by the Hoadley Company of Australia: Violet Crumble—a bar of honeycomb coated with milk chocolate, and Polly Waffle—a hollow bar of milk-chocolate-coated cereal (something like rice crispies) filled with a light, fluffy marshmallow. When we were kids, we had most fun with Jaffas—chocolate balls covered with orange candy. They make a loud noise when dropped on the wooden floors of movie theaters. Cherry Ripes also take a lot of beating.

DOT BOWMANS

The legendary Dot Bowman of Dandenong produced this when we asked for a specially good cookie recipe for a cookbook our local school was assembling.

½ cup (1 stick) butter
¼ cup sugar
1 cup chopped dates
3 cups Rice Krispies
½ to 1 cup chocolate chips, melted

- Place butter, sugar, and dates in saucepan and stir over low heat until a thick paste forms. Put Rice Krispies in large bowl, add date mixture, and stir well. Spread in a shallow pan. Cover with melted chocolate. Cool in refrigerator and cut into 1 ½-inch squares.

Makes 12 squares.

ABOUT DANDENONG: Dandenong is one of our spouse's hometown. It's nothing like the name suggests (a sleepy dusty village in the red of the Australian outback). Not at all. It's a bustling city, part of the suburban sprawl of Melbourne (located on the southeastern tip of Australia). Australia folklore authority Keith McKenry reports that "Dandenong" is aboriginal for "no good damper" which must be what aborigines many years ago thought of the cooking in this area!

"Damper wrong! Damper wrong!"
The toothless blacks all cried,
Excepting those who'd swallowed some,
And they laid down and died.
For what they'd gone and done, you see,
Though flour had been meant,

They'd gone and pinched a hundredweight
Of best Portland cement
Now over the years that mournful cry
Of *Damper Wrong* has changed,
And this is how the district
Of Dandenong got its name.
—*"How Dandenong Got Its Name," Keith McKenry, 1970*

FROSTED CHERRY ROUNDS

1 egg
¾ cup flour
2 tablespoons rice flour
½ cup fine sugar
½ cup (1 stick) butter
⅓ cup coconut
2 tablespoons candied cherries

- Separate egg yolk and white. Sift flour and rice flour; add ½ cup of the sugar and rub in butter and add egg yolk until mixture forms a stiff dough. Turn onto board and knead lightly. Roll out to 1 inch thickness. Cut into 1-inch rounds with fluted cutter and place on greased cookie sheet.

Whip egg white stiffly and add remaining ½ cup sugar and the coconut. Pile this mixture onto cookies and top with cherry. Preheat oven to 350 degrees, place in oven, reset oven to 300 degrees, and bake for 20 to 25 minutes, or until coconut is brown. *Makes 12.*

JEAN'S GINGER SLICE

This is another prize recipe from Dandenong (pronounced Dan-dee-nong; see Dot Bowmans, page 158). These slices will keep well, stored in an airtight container in refrigerator.

¾ cup (1 ½ sticks) butter

1 ¾ cups flour

¼ teaspoon salt

1 cup fine sugar

½ cup preserved ginger, chopped

1 egg

- Melt butter in saucepan and allow to cool. Add remaining ingredients, mixing thoroughly. Spread in shallow 10-inch pan and bake in 350-degree oven for 25 minutes. Allow to cool in pan, cut into slices.

Makes 12.

MAY'S FUDGE SHORTBREAD

½ cup (1 stick) butter
½ cup sugar
1 ½ cups flour

- Beat together butter and sugar. Add flour until mixture is firm enough to roll and put in shallow pan. Cook at 375 degrees for 15 minutes.

½ cup (1 stick) butter
½ cup fine sugar
4 tablespoons golden syrup*
1 cup condensed milk

- Place all ingredients in bowl and beat until creamy. Cook in small saucepan over medium heat, until mixture bubbles. Let cool, spread over shortbread. Allow to cool, then add topping:

2 ounces dark chocolate
2 tablespoons butter

- Melt chocolate, add butter and mix thoroughly. Pour over milk mixture, allow to cool, then cut into slices for serving. *Makes 12.*

*ABOUT GOLDEN SYRUP: Golden syrup is a byproduct of molasses manufacture and is hard to find in America, though should be available at your gourmet food store. We have substituted 1 part light and 1 part dark corn syrup with some success, although this mixture tends not to have the strong sugary-sweetness of golden syrup.

ORANGE (LEMON) FINGERS

½ cup (1 stick) butter
⅓ cup condensed milk
6 cups coconut
½ pound plain cookies, crumbled
rind of 1 orange
orange icing (page 215, substitute orange in Lemon Icing)

- Heat butter and condensed milk over low heat. Add to dry ingredients. Mix well, press into shallow pan, then top with orange icing (or use lemon icing, made with lemon flavoring).

Makes 2 dozen.

RASPBERRY SANDWICHES

½ cup (1 stick) butter
¾ cup sugar
1 egg
2 cups flour
1 teaspoon cream of tartar
½ teaspoon baking soda
raspberry jam

- Cream butter and sugar, add egg and beat well. Sift together flour, cream of tartar, and baking soda. Add to butter mixture and mix well. Roll out ¼ inch thick and cut into 2-inch circles. Bake in a 400-degree oven for 5 to 10 minutes. While hot, cut rounds in half and join together with jam.

Makes 12.

BURNT BUTTER BISCUITS (COOKIES)

1 cup (2 sticks) butter
1 cup sugar
2 eggs
1 teaspoon vanilla
1 ¼ cups self-rising flour
1 pinch salt
16 almonds

- Brown the butter, being careful not to burn it. Allow it to cool then cream with sugar. Add eggs, then vanilla, sifted flour, and salt. Place small teaspoonfuls on cookie tray, and place half an almond on top of each. Bake 10 minutes at 375 degrees.

Makes 12 to 16.

LEMON SNAPS

1 cup sugar
1 egg
½ cup (1 stick) butter
2 lemons for juice, rind of one
flour to stiffen

- Mix all ingredients together thoroughly, adding flour to stiffen to desired consistency. Roll out thin, place on cookie tray, and bake in a 400-degree oven about 7 minutes.

Makes 12 two-inch squares.

NEENISH TARTS

½ cup butter
½ cup sugar
1 egg
1 cup flour
1 teaspoon baking powder
1 pinch salt

- Cream butter and sugar, add egg and beat well. Mix in sifted dry ingredients and knead well. Roll out thin, cut into circles a little larger than muffin cups. Line greased muffin pans with the mixture. Prick with fork and bake 10 to 15 minutes at 350 degrees. Now prepare filling:

½ cup (1 stick) butter
½ cup fine sugar
½ cup condensed milk
2 tablespoons lemon juice

Vanilla icing (page 214)
Chocolate icing (page 215)

- Soften butter, add sugar, condensed milk, and lemon juice. Spoon into baked patty shells. When set, ice top, half with vanilla icing and half with chocolate icing.
Makes 12.

ROMA'S CHOCOLATE VELVET

1 ½ cups finely crushed chocolate cookies
⅓ cup melted butter

- Mix together cookies and butter and press into 9- x 13-inch flat pan. Bake at 325 degrees for 10 minutes. Cool.

1 (8 ounce) package cream cheese
½ cup sugar
1 teaspoon vanilla (or less)
2 eggs, separated
1 (6 ounce) package chocolate chips, melted
1 cup whipped cream
¾ cup chopped walnuts

- Combine softened cream cheese, ½ cup sugar, and vanilla, mixing well. Stir in beaten egg yolks and chocolate. Beat egg whites until stiff peaks form. Gradually beat in remaining ½ cup of sugar. Fold in whipped cream and nuts; pour over cookie crumbs. Freeze. When frozen, remove and cut into 1-inch squares for serving.

Makes 12 squares.

AUTHENTIC AUSTRALIAN? There's always a question of whether certain recipes are authentically Australian or not, especially because just about everyone in Australia (except the Aborigines, and even *they* came from Asia some 40,000 years ago) came there from some place else. Frankly, this recipe looks very American to us—the cream cheese is a bit of a give-away. But it's one that we've had for a long time, given to us by one of our moms. It's so delicious, we couldn't resist including it.

Chapter 9

Cakes

C akes, as with cookies, are always present in the Australian kitchen. The necessity to keep cakes and cookies in
supply is what sets the Australian kitchen apart from its American counterpart. It is usually cluttered with all kinds of containers for storing cakes and cookies. There are different
containers for different cakes. Those with pastry in them
should not be in completely airtight containers. Light cakes,
however, such as sponges need to be completely airtight or
they will dry out.

Cakes are most often served for "afternoon tea" which may be
anywhere from 2:00 p.m. to 4:00 p.m. While some work places
stop for afternoon tea, it is not a common practice. Afternoon tea
is more likely to be served to guests who arrive in the afternoon
during a weekend visit. Usually, these guests are invited or
expected, and baking is done specially in preparation for them.
One mom liked to cook a tea cake just as guests arrived, so that
it could be taken out of the oven and eaten straight away.

Afternoon tea is not to be confused with the Scottish practice
of taking "High Tea" on Sundays. This is a combined afternoon
tea and evening meal, at which are served savories, eggs, toast,
along with a variety of cakes and jellies. High tea is not served
in Australia. However, to confuse matters, the word "tea time" is
used by many Australians to refer to the evening meal.

AMY JOHNSTON CAKE

Pastry, cakes, and jam—these simple favorites are put together and topped with lemon or vanilla frosting to make this delicious cake. It will excite the taste buds of even sworn beer drinkers.*

Pastry:
4 tablespoons butter
½ cup self-rising flour
¼ cup of milk (approx.)
1 jar (10 ounces) raspberry jam

- Rub butter into flour, adding enough milk to make a fairly stiff paste. Roll pastry about 8 x 8 inches, place in 8-inch pan and spread with jam.

Cake:
1 cup self-rising flour
1 cup sugar
4 tablespoons butter
2 eggs
½ cup milk
Vanilla or lemon icing (page 214/215)

- Blend flour and sugar, rub in butter. Stir eggs lightly, add to mixture, blend while adding enough milk to make a smooth consistency—easy to stir but not too thin. Pour over jam and bake 25 minutes at 350 degrees. Top with icing when cold. Cut into 2-inch squares and serve with English tea**.
Makes about 24 squares.

*A genuine Aussie beer drinker (an "Ocka") would never admit to eating cakes or cookies. A real Aussie beer drinker doesn't eat sweets. He drinks beer and eats meat pies (see Pie 'n Sauce, Chapter 2).

**Well...there are lots of Aussies who, in their small rebellious way, now drink coffee—and be damned to the English! We've tried Amy Johnston cake with American coffee, and can tell you it's terrific. However, if you plan to prepare tea, Australians are very particular about how it's made (whereas the English are more concerned with how one holds the cup!). See *cuppa tea*, page 225.

MAISIE'S CHOCOLATE PEPPERMINT CAKE

½ cup (1 stick) butter
½ cup sugar
2 eggs
½ teaspoon vanilla
⅔ cup self-rising flour
4 tablespoons cocoa
water to mix

- Cream butter and sugar. Add well beaten eggs and vanilla. Fold in flour and cocoa, mixing to a thick creamy consistency by adding water. Place in 9-inch cake pan. Bake in 350-degree oven for 30 minutes. When cool, slice horizontally and insert filling. Or, better yet cook another one, and place on top of the first, with filling between.

Peppermint filling:
2 tablespoons butter
¼ cup fine sugar
1 tablespoon hot water
1 tablespoon milk
3 to 6 drops peppermint extract
green food coloring
chocolate icing (page 215)

- Cream butter and sugar, add hot water, mix again, then add milk, peppermint extract, and food coloring. Mix until creamy and smooth. Now a final touch. Cover the entire cake with a thick chocolate icing.

Makes one 9-inch cake.

HELEN'S CHOCOLATE CAKE

1 cup self-rising flour
1 cup sugar
4 tablespoons cocoa powder
5 ½ tablespoons butter
½ cup milk
2 eggs
chocolate icing (page 215)

* Put flour, sugar, and cocoa in a bowl. Melt butter, add ½ cup of the milk. Add eggs and melted butter to dry ingredients and beat well. Add the remaining ½ cup milk as needed until a firm batter is made. Put into a floured and lined 9-inch cake pan and bake in a 350-degree oven for 20 minutes. Press center of cake to test. If it springs back it is done. Cool on a wire rack and ice with good chocolate icing. This is a very simple and easy cake to make and can be dressed up by adding golden raisins, coconut, chopped nuts, or served with ice cream as dessert.

Makes one 9-inch cake.

APPLE SHORTCAKE

½ cup (1 stick) butter
½ cup fine sugar
1 egg
1 cup self-rising flour
1 teaspoon each, cinnamon, ginger, and allspice
2 unsweetened stewed apples
confectioners' sugar (optional)

- Cream butter and sugar, add egg, then dry ingredients. Spread mixture into two greased and floured 9-inch cake tins. Do not spread right to the edge and you will get a nice flat top on the cakes. Bake in a 350-degree oven for about 30 minutes. They will be light brown and crisp when cooked. The shortcake can be made many days before you wish to use it and only needs 2 hours to soften after filling. Put the stewed apples between the cakes about 2 hours before serving. Sprinkle top with confectioners' sugar or spread with whipped cream. Other fillings can be used such as strawberries or pitted prunes folded through whipped cream.

Makes one 9-inch cake.

MARSHMALLOW CAKE

We can understand how it might be assumed that any cake or cookie with marshmallow in it would be as American as apple pie! For this recipe you get to make your own marshmallow.

½ cup (1 stick) butter
½ cup sugar
1 egg
rind of 1 lemon, grated
1 cup self-rising flour

- Cream butter and sugar, add egg and lemon rind. Fold in flour. Press into 8-inch pan and bake at 350 degrees for 15 minutes or until golden brown. When cool, make topping:

1 tablespoon gelatin
1 cup sugar
¾ cup water
lemon juice
coconut

- Place gelatin, sugar, and water into saucepan, bring slowly to simmer. Allow to cool, place in refrigerator for half an hour or until quite cold. Beat until thick and white, add lemon juice to taste. Spread over cake, top with coconut.

Makes 2 dozen 2-inch squares.

ABOUT MARSHMALLOW IN AUSTRALIA: Marshmallow enjoys a warm spot in every expatriate Australian's heart. Most Aussies have never seen snow, but they do know that light fluffy marshmallow in "snowballs" (a ball of marshmallow dipped in chocolate) is whiter than snow, and is one of the memorable Aussie lollies (candy). The word "candy" is not commonly used in Australia. Every kid asks for "lollies." Strangely, this word is often used in another context; "to shoot the lolly" is to lose one's temper.

SPONGE CAKE

In our parents' time, an accomplished cook was judged by how well she could make a sponge cake. These cakes are possibly the most typical of old-fashioned Australian cooking. The recipes look simple enough, but be warned, it is especially difficult to achieve the light and airy consistency that sets this cake apart from all other cakes. Here is one of our mom's favorites.

1 cup flour
¾ cup sugar
3 eggs
6 tablespoons butter, melted
4 tablespoons milk
2 teaspoons baking powder

- In a bowl, put flour and sugar, break in eggs, add melted butter and milk. Beat 3 minutes, then stir in baking powder. Pour into two greased 8-inch cake pans and bake at 375 degrees for 15 to 20 minutes. Sponges are typically served with jam and whipped cream in the center, sometimes with frosting on the top. A very popular version is to cover the cake with thick whipped cream and decorate with strawberries. By all means serve this with a nice cup of tea! (see cuppa tea, page 225).

Makes a two-layer 8-inch cake.

ABOUT COOKING SPONGE (PRONOUNCED SPUNJ) CAKE: There are many stories that purport to explain the failures of cooking sponge cake. We still believe that slamming a door loudly at precisely the wrong moment while the sponge is in the oven will cause it to collapse, or fail to rise. There's no greater embarrassment than to retrieve a flat sponge from the oven! However, thanks to another Australian favorite, there's something wonderful you can do to camouflage a fallen sponge.... you can turn it into lamingtons. Read on!

LEMON SPONGE

1 lemon
4 eggs
1 cup sugar
½ cup self-rising flour

• Grate rind of whole lemon, but extract juice from only ½ of the lemon. Separate egg whites from yolks. Beat whites stiffly, adding sugar gradually. Add egg yolks and beat until thick and creamy. Fold in flour, rind, and juice. Grease one 9-inch cake pan and place wax paper in bottom. Pour mixture into pan and bake at 375 degrees for about 15 minutes.

Makes one (9-inch) layer cake.

LAMINGTONS

These cakes are named after Lord Lamington, governor of Queensland, 1895-1901, and are by far the most popular Australian cake. They are found at tea parties and social gatherings—especially those of church groups. Lamingtons are that close to being sacred! The wonderful thing about lamingtons is that, provided one has the sponge cake, one can produce these classics with hardly any effort.

1 recipe sponge cake (page 174)
chocolate icing (page 215)
flaked coconut

- Prepare the sponge cake batter, and pour into well-greased 8- x 12-inch pan, so that mixture is approximately ¾ inch deep. Bake at 350 degrees for 15 to 20 minutes. When cake has cooled, cut into approximately 2-inch squares. Prepare lots of chocolate icing. Dip each square in chocolate icing, then sprinkle all over with coconut. You won't believe how this simple recipe will send your guests absolutely nuts! And your kids who insist that they don't like coconut, will suddenly discover that they love it!

VARIATION: Instead of chocolate icing, dip squares in strawberry or raspberry Jell-O, and sprinkle with coconut. These are a little more messy, and should be eaten right away.
Makes 2 dozen 2-inch squares.

ABOUT SPONGE CAKE IN AMERICA: We have searched many bake shops in the American northeast for cake that is similar to sponge cake, but have had no success. In Australia, one can buy a slab of "golden sponge" which saves having to make the cake. We have tried this recipe with slabs of "plain" cake and angel food cake, with reasonable results. It's hard to beat the real thing, but even this substitution produces terrific lamingtons.

TEA CAKE

This is a light plain cake, often served with a cup of tea (see cuppa tea, page 225) in the afternoon. When we were kids, we used to hang around the kitchen and try to convince our mom to let us have a slice as soon as the cake came out of the oven.

2 tablespoons butter
½ cup sugar
1 egg
½ cup milk
1 ½ cups self-rising flour

Topping:
Butter
Sugar
Cinnamon

- Cream butter and sugar. Add egg, then milk and flour. Pour into well greased 9-inch cake pan and bake 25 minutes at 350 degrees. While still hot, rub butter on top and sprinkle with cinnamon and sugar. If there is any left the next day, try slices spread with butter, accompanied by a cup of tea, of course.

Makes one 9-inch cake.

AUTHENTICALLY AUSTRALIAN? There is, admittedly, a question as to just how Australian this particular cake is. Tea cake is popular in England, where, after all, the tradition of afternoon teas originated. We certainly have a lot to thank the Poms for! "Pommies" or "Poms" are what Australians call the English. The word "Limey," common in America, is rarely used. In an Australian pub the English are more likely to be referred to as "whinging (pronounced win-jing) bloody Poms" which means that they complain all the time.

DATE AND APPLE TEA CAKE

4 tablespoons butter
½ cup sugar
1 egg
1 cup Bran Buds cereal
¾ cup milk
1 ¼ cups self-rising flour
1 pinch salt
1 cup chopped dates
1 grated apple
lemon icing (page 215)
dates and nuts for garnish

- Cream butter and sugar, add egg and beat well. Stir in bran buds, milk, sifted flour, and salt, mixing all together lightly. Spread half the mixture in a greased 9-inch pan and cover with dates and apple. Spread the remaining cake mixture on top and bake for 30 minutes at 375 degrees. Cover warm cake with lemon icing and sprinkle with chopped dates and nuts.

Makes one 9-inch cake.

BANANA TEA CAKE

4 tablespoons butter
½ cup sugar
1 egg
½ cup milk
1 ½ cups self-rising flour
½ teaspoon baking powder
1 banana

- Cream butter and sugar, then add egg, milk, flour and baking soda. Mash banana and mix into ingredients. Pour into a greased 9-inch pan. Bake in a 375-degree oven for 25 minutes.

Makes one 9-inch cake.

ORANGE CAKE

Australia's temperate climate ensures that there is plentiful supply of fruit, almost year-round. Oranges and lemons are among the favorites. Lemons turn up in slices and fillings. Oranges are found in many cakes.

½ cup (1 stick) butter
⅔ cup sugar
2 eggs
rind of one orange
½ cup milk
2 cups self-rising flour
lemon icing (page 215, substitute orange in Lemon Icing)

- Beat butter and sugar together, add eggs one at a time, then orange rind. Add milk and flour and beat for 1 minute. Pour into a greased 9-inch pan. Bake at 400 degrees for 45 minutes. Make lemon icing but substitute orange for lemon.

Makes one 9-inch cake.

APPLE CAKE

½ cup (1 stick) butter
½ cup sugar
1 egg
1 ½ cups self-rising flour
1 cup flour
2 teaspoons cocoa
2 teaspoons cinnamon
1 cup milk
1 teaspoon baking soda, dissolved in 4 teaspoons water
1 cup apple sauce
chocolate icing (page 215)

- Cream butter and sugar, add egg. Sift flours, cocoa, and cinnamon. Add to the butter mixture, alternating with milk. Mix baking soda into applesauce, and add this to flour mixture. Pour into a greased 9-inch pan. Cook in 350-degree oven for 40 minutes. Top with chocolate icing. This is a deliciously moist spicy cake. Plan to eat it the day you cook it as it is does not keep well.

Makes one 9-inch cake.

The cynical reader may have been waiting to come across an Australian recipe for apple pie, since we have included many other recipes that seem to be just as common in England as in Australia. But we couldn't be that brazen, even though Australia boasts a state, Tasmania, popularly called the "Apple Isle." There are Australian recipes for apple pie, but they do not vary from the American versions.

FAIRY CAKES

Children the world over love miniatures of all kinds. American kids love cupcakes, standard fare at birthday parties. Not to be outdone, Australian kids have their equivalent, with a little more fanciful name, Fairy Cakes. When we were little, our moms made lots of these, though the practice then was to serve them plain, or perhaps cut open and filled with a little raspberry jam. These days, it's unusual to see them without frosting.

½ cup self-rising flour
½ cup cornstarch
2 eggs
1 teaspoon vanilla extract
½ cup (1 stick) butter
½ cup sugar

- Thoroughly mix all ingredients together. Spoon into small muffin pans or into paper muffin cups. Bake in 325-degree oven for 15 minutes.

VARIATION: To make Butterfly Cakes, slice top off each cake and cut the slice in half. Top cake with whipped cream and sprinkle with red Jell-O. Insert the two halves of the slice into the topping to make the butterfly wings.

Makes 12 cakes.

DREAM CAKE

1 ½ cups flour
1 teaspoon baking soda
½ cup (1 stick) butter
½ cup fine sugar
rind of 1 orange
2 eggs
¼ cup golden syrup*
1 ½ teaspoons baking powder
½ cup currants
½ cup raisins
½ cup chopped nuts
juice of 1 orange

- Sift flour and baking soda. Beat butter, sugar, and little flour together; add orange rind. Separate egg yolks from whites. Beat whites, gradually adding golden syrup. Add yolks, then flour and butter mixture. Beat in baking powder along with remaining flour. Fold in currants, raisins, and nuts; add orange juice. Pour into well-greased 9-inch cake pan, bake at 350 degrees for about 1 ½ hours.

Makes one 9-inch cake.

*ABOUT GOLDEN SYRUP: See page 162 for notes on possible substitutes. ½ cup brown sugar could be substituted for the golden syrup in this recipe. It will taste O.K., but without golden syrup you will never know what Dream Cake *really* tastes like.

We don't know exactly where these cakes got their name, perhaps because their creator dreamed about them. But they do give us an excuse to mention the *Dream Time* in Aboriginal folklore. The Aborigines, even though they had been separated into hundreds of completely separate tribes in ancient times, believe generally that they originated about 40,000 years ago. At that time, all animals were giants that behaved like humans.

Many stories tell of their exploits which often explain how rivers were formed and mountains were made. The period is known as *Dream Time*. At some elusive point in time, and for reasons unknown, the giants became humans, and the *Dream Time* ended.

FUDGE CAKE

10 tablespoons butter
2 tablespoons golden syrup (page 162)
1 cup self-rising flour
2 tablespoons cocoa
1 cup crushed cornflakes
½ cup sugar
1 cup coconut
chocolate icing (page 215)

* Melt butter and golden syrup, add to dry ingredients. Press into flat 9-inch pan and bake about 10 minutes at 375 degrees. Top with chocolate icing.

Makes one 9-inch cake.

WHITE CHRISTMAS CAKE

4 ounces (½ cup) glacé cherries
4 ounces (½ cup) glacé pineapple
2 ounces (¼ cup) glacé figs
2 ounces (¼ cup) glacé apricots
2 ounces (¼ cup) mixed candied peel
4 ounces (½ cup) preserved ginger
½ cup walnuts
2 tablespoons honey
2 tablespoons marmalade
2 teaspoons grated lemon rind
¼ cup sweet sherry
½ teaspoon glycerin
1 teaspoon vanilla
1 cup (2 sticks) butter
1 cup fine sugar
4 eggs
2 ¾ cups flour
1 teaspoon ground ginger

Halve cherries and chop remaining fruit and walnuts coarsely. Combine in bowl with honey, marmalade, lemon rind, sherry, glycerin, and vanilla. Cover and allow to stand overnight. Beat butter until soft, add sugar, beating until light and creamy. Add eggs one at a time making sure to beat well after each egg. Add to fruit mixture, mix well, and stir in sifted flour and ginger. Line a deep 10-inch cake pan with several layers of wax paper then spread mixture evenly into pan. Bake in 275 to 300-degree oven for 2 ½ hours.
Makes one 10-inch cake.

ARE THESE CAKES TRULY AUSTRALIAN? We have to admit, we don't know. Yes, the tradition of rich fruit cakes, puddings, and tarts using dried and candied fruits comes from England (which our dad has always referred to as "the old country"). After all, Australia was settled mainly by the English, though later than North America. Captain Cook set foot on Australia's shores in 1772, around the time of the American Revolution. Thanks to the rebellious Americans, England had to find somewhere else to send her convicts, and Australia was it: an unintended byproduct of the American Revolution!

Thank you again, America!

CANDIED FRUIT CAKE DELUXE

1 cup flour
1 teaspoon baking powder
6 ounces seeded raisins
4 ounces golden raisins
8 ounces whole glacé cherries
4 ounces chopped dates
4 ounces glacé apricots
6 ounces stoned prunes
½ pound glacé pineapple (coarsely chopped)
2 eggs
½ cup brandy
½ cup sugar
1 ¼ pounds whole nuts (brazils and almonds)

- Sift flour and baking powder, then sift onto the mixed fruit and toss lightly. Beat the eggs with brandy and sugar until frothy; add to fruit mixture. Mix in nuts until evenly distributed and coated. Grease and line a 10-inch tube pan with wax paper and fill. Press down firmly with wetted hands and decorate the top with cherries and nuts. Bake at 325 degrees for 1 ½ hours and cool in pan.

- While fruit cake addicts prefer their cake "straight," others like the cake topped with a rich apricot glaze:

Apricot glaze:
2 tablespoons sugar
1 tablespoon water
4 tablespoons strained apricot jam

- Place sugar, water and jam in small pan. Bring slowly to a boil and stir until sugar dissolves. Simmer gently for 2 minutes, then, while cake is still hot, brush liberally with glaze. Leave in pan to cool.

Makes one 10-inch tube cake.

DAD'S FRUIT CAKE

½ pound mixed candied fruit
½ pound dark raisins
½ pound golden raisins
½ cup sherry
1 cup (2 sticks) butter
½ cup brown sugar
4 eggs
2 ½ cups self-rising flour
1 ½ teaspoons cinnamon
pinch of salt

- Stir together mixed fruit, dark and golden raisins and sherry. Let it stand. Cream butter and sugar, adding each egg separately. Add flour, cinnamon, and salt and beat well in electric mixer. Remove from mixer, and fold in fruit by hand. Grease 8-inch pan and place mixture in it—mixture will be stiff and heavy to work. Place in oven and bake at 275 to 300 degrees for 2 hours.

Makes one 8-inch cake.

ABOUT FRUIT CAKE IN AUSTRALIA: Fruit cake is, of course, *the* cake of England, and is especially common at Christmastime. It is very popular because it keeps a long time (we have heard of some that has kept for years!). The reason it keeps so long is the sherry, which may be substituted with any fortified wine, or in this recipe 1 tablespoon brandy.

MANGO CHEESECAKE

Crumb crust:
1 cup plain cookie crumbs (graham crackers)
1 cup finely chopped pecans or walnuts
5 tablespoons butter, melted

Cream cheese filling:
4 ounces cream cheese
½ cup fine sugar
3 medium mangoes, chopped
1 small carton (1 cup) heavy cream
2 tablespoons gelatin
¼ cup hot water

- Combine crumbs, nuts, and butter in bowl, mix well. Press evenly over base of greased 9-inch springform pan and refrigerate for 30 minutes.

- Blend cream cheese, sugar, and half the mango until smooth. Add cream, blend until combined. Transfer mixture to large bowl. Sprinkle gelatin over hot water; cool, but do not allow mixture to set. Add gelatin to mango mixture, stir in remaining mangoes.

- Pour filling over cookie base, refrigerate several hours or until set.

Makes one 9-inch cheesecake.

Chapter 10

Desserts

Australia cannot boast as many authentically Australian desserts as it can cookies and cakes. Some of its puddings are, of course, English in origin. However, their popularity is so strong, and they have been adapted to Australian ingredients in many cases, that it is reasonable to think of them as Australian. This observation applies especially to steamed puddings.

Two desserts deserve special mention, however. These are Pavlova and Peach Melba. They are special because they do not appear to be as directly derivative of our English heritage, and because they are named after famous stage performers who toured Australia at the turn of the century. Pavlova was a famous Russian ballet dancer, and Dame Nellie Melba a famous Australian opera singer. We wonder whether there is any historical significance to the naming of these desserts after such people. Perhaps it could begin a tradition. Other famous people could inspire such sweets as Reagan Roll, Pears Major, Thatcher-in-the-Pie, Bananas Buchanan, or Clinton Rolly Polly. Need we go on?

It is often bluntly, sometimes gruffly, stated that real Aussie men (that is, the ones that drink gallons of beer, curse at the footy umpire (referee), and eat pies 'n sauce) don't eat sweets (an Australian term for desserts). This is a blatant lie. We have seen many of them do so, though rarely, it is true, in a bar. They couldn't do that anyway, because no publican (i.e. hotel keeper) in his right mind would even suggest such a thing, though he might serve sweets in the "Ladies Lounge" (see Drinks and Drinking, Chapter 12).

FRUIT JELLY (JELL-O)

Australian kids call Jell-O and its equivalents "jelly." There are many variations of this recipe, but one thing is certain: jelly is a perennial kids' favorite.

2 packets (4-serving size) Jell-O (different colors)
1 to 2 cups diced fruit
1 ½ cups milk
1 tablespoon gelatin
1 tablespoon sugar
3 to 6 drops vanilla (to taste)

* Australia is blessed with a temperate climate, so fresh fruit is abundant. Try to use fresh fruit (except pineapple) if you can, but canned fruit will do (drain before use). Prepare one packet of Jell-O, mixing in diced fruit. Allow to set. Make white jelly by heating milk, almost to a boil, and adding gelatin, sugar, and vanilla. Stir until all ingredients are dissolved. Spoon onto fruit Jell-O. Allow to set. Mix second packet of Jell-O, pour on top. Allow to set, cut in squares to serve.

Makes 12 servings.

FRUIT SALAD

This is Australia's most popular summertime dessert. The abundance of fresh fruits ensures that the dish will never fail, and it's so easy to prepare. The serious host would go to the green grocer (a disappearing breed who is not green but rather specializes in selling all kinds of vegetables and fruits) and hand pick all fruits. These might include (but are not limited to) grapes, peaches, pears, apples, oranges, strawberries, and bananas. The bananas should be added last and soaked in lemon juice before adding, to delay browning. Add sugar to taste, though if you have selected your fruits carefully, there should be just enough natural sweetness. Fruit salad is most often served with ice cream.

BRANDIED FRUIT SALAD

1 (16 ounce) can red cherries
1 (16 ounce) can pineapple pieces
1 (16 ounce) can sliced peaches
1 cup sugar
½ cup dark raisins
½ cup golden raisins
1 cup stoned chopped prunes
1 cup brandy

- Strain juice off canned fruits. Place juice into an enamel or Pyrex saucepan. Add sugar, dark and golden raisins, and prunes. Bring to boil then simmer for 10 minutes. Add canned fruits and brandy. Place in an airtight jar(s) and leave in the refrigerator for three weeks. Serve with whipped cream or ice cream. This is served at Christmastime in Australia. Other dried fruits such as apricots, can be added, but the variety of colors is an important consideration.

Serves 8 to 10.

PAVLOVA

In any season of the year, at any party, this renowned Australian dessert will be served. A kind of giant meringue, each spoonful of Pavlova instantly dissolves in the mouth. The wonderful thing is that, because Pavlova can be prepared in many different ways, one can always be surprised at a new and delightful variation.

Pavlovas can be difficult to cook unless you know a couple of tricks. Don't have the oven too hot. 275 degrees is plenty. Don't over-beat the mixture or the egg whites will toughen, and the Pavlova will shrink too much when cooking. Pavlovas do not keep well. Plan to cook on the day you will serve it.

The variations in Pavlovas are achieved mostly by different fillings. The preferred fillings are mounds of whipped cream mixed with fresh fruit in some of the following combinations:

sliced banana and passion fruit
fresh raspberries and pineapple
fresh strawberries and pineapple
fruit salad (page 195)

- If you're inclined, the addition of cordials (called *liqueurs* in Australia) such as Cointreau, orange curaçao, or even a little Cognac to the appropriate fruits gives the old taste buds an extra kick.

- The greatest joy (besides eating it) is the sight of the magnificent Pavlova rising up from the table like a huge snowball. Baked Alaska pales into insignificance beside it. Because it's so popular and there are some important variations in cooking method, we have included a few of the most interesting.

MOM'S PAVLOVA

3 to 4 egg whites
1 cup fine sugar
1 pinch salt
2 tablespoons cornstarch
½ teaspoon cream of tartar
1 teaspoon vanilla extract
1 teaspoon vinegar

- Beat egg whites until stiff, add sifted dry ingredients, then add vanilla and vinegar. Line a 10-inch greased cake pan with wax paper, spoon in mixture. Bake at 275 degrees for 1 ½ hours. Allow to cool, fill with preferred filling.

Makes one 10-inch Pavlova.

ROSEMARY'S PAVLOVA

This recipe allows you to choose how big you would like to make your Pavlova, using relative quantities.

egg whites
⅓ cup sugar to each egg white
1 teaspoon cornstarch to each egg white
½ teaspoon vinegar to each egg white
½ teaspoon vanilla to each egg white
confectioners' sugar and cornstarch for pan

- Beat eggs until stiff, then add sugar gradually, beating all the time. Fold in cornstarch and vinegar. On cookie tray, sprinkle equal parts cornstarch and confectioners' sugar. Make a 2- to 3-inch-high circular collar of aluminum foil and place on baking tray. Spoon in egg white mixture. Place in a 325-degree oven for 30 minutes, then reduce heat to 275 degrees for 1 more hour. Top with favorite filling.

Four egg whites make a 10-inch Pavlova.

COFFEE PAVLOVA

4 egg whites
1 pinch salt
1 ½ cups sugar
1 tablespoon cornstarch
1 teaspoon instant coffee powder
1 teaspoon vinegar
confectioners' sugar and cornstarch for pan

Filling:
½ pint whipped cream
1 tablespoon coffee powder
1 tablespoon Tia Maria or rum (if you must!)
grated chocolate, for garnish

- Place egg whites and salt in clean, warm dry bowl and beat until stiff. Gradually beat in ¾ cup sugar, adding to the mixture a tablespoon at a time, and beating well after each addition. Beat until thick and glossy. Now fold in remaining ¾ cup sugar. Quickly add cornstarch, coffee, and vinegar. On an overturned 9-inch cake pan, sprinkle equal parts cornstarch and confectioners' sugar. Tie a band of greased aluminum foil around pan, 3 inches high. Spoon in mixture, bake at 300 degrees for 1 ¼ hours. When cold, mix filling. Mix whipped cream with coffee powder and Tia Maria. Top with grated chocolate.

Makes one 10- to 12-inch Pavlova.

CHRISTMAS PUDDING

Though it might be hot on Christmas day, and some Australians have been known to have Christmas dinner on the beach, there are few who would allow Christmas to pass without hot Christmas pudding. All Christmas puddings are a variation of what the English call Plum Pudding, although there are no plums in the mixture.

Christmas pudding is a special favorite of both old and young. The grown-ups look forward to Christmas Pudding because it is terrific with Brandy Cream (page 214).

The kids can hardly contain themselves, because Christmas pudding is always served with small coins hidden inside! (Only silver coins are used, which in Australia are 5, 10, and 20 cent pieces, though the 20 cent pieces are a bit large for this.) Yes, it can be dangerous, and we have known kids who have swallowed the 5 cent pieces (the smallest coin) and had to be rushed to the doctor. But nothing ever happens, not even a tummy ache. However, if you decide to try your hand at this fun tradition, we suggest that you issue several warnings to your excited guests, adults as well as kids. Also, in the olden days when coins were pure silver (or close to it) the coins were cooked right in the pudding. This is no longer a good idea because the alloys in the coins will leave a nasty taste! Boil the coins separately, then just before serving the pudding, order everyone out of the kitchen, and wedge the coins into the pudding. With a little care, one can hide coins so they cannot be seen too easily—although the kids are pretty hard to fool.

There are a lot of different traditions in families in regard to what to hide in the pudding. We know of one strange family that hid a bone button in the pudding. The person who got it was said to have a poor year the next year! So much for good will to all men!

LIL'S PLUM PUDDING

3 cups flour
1 cup sugar
½ pound (1 cup) dark raisins
½ pound (1 cup) currants
½ pound (1 cup) golden raisins
3 dates
1 tablespoon mixed candied peel
¼ teaspoon ginger
¼ teaspoon cloves
1 tablespoon cinnamon
2 teaspoons allspice
½ teaspoon nutmeg
2 cups boiling water
½ cup (1 stick) butter
2 teaspoons baking soda
brandy to taste

- Mix flour, sugar, fruits, peel, brandy, and spices in a bowl. Put boiling water in a saucepan with butter. When it boils add baking soda, 1 teaspoon at a time. (Watch carefully, as it may froth over.) Mix the wet with the dry and put into a greased and floured ovenproof bowl. Make a lid of two layers of waxed paper, fasten with string around bowl's rim. Place in a saucepan and boil 4 hours. Keep level of boiling water about ¾ the way up the pudding bowl. When cool, keep in airtight container in refrigerator for up to 6 weeks. Serves 8.

Plum puddings are best made well ahead of time. They actually improve with age (we have made extra quantities and eaten them the following Christmas!). To reheat, place in boiling water as before, simmer for 1 hour.

Christmas pudding is usually served with a small sprig of holly inserted in the top of the pudding after it has been emptied out onto a decorative plate. Allow your eager guests to choose from store-bought brandy sauce, Brandy Cream (page 214), whipped cream, or vanilla ice cream as toppings.

If you're lucky enough to have any left over, sneak down to the kitchen early in the morning on Boxing Day (the day after Christmas), and cut yourself a thin cold slice. Fry it in a little butter, or simply eat it cold with a warm cup of milk coffee. It makes the breakfast of the year!

RED CAPS

Steamed puddings are *very* English, of course. Not to be outdone, though, we Australians have managed to produce a variation on the theme. Red Caps are little steam puddings, cooked in small tea cups, so that each person receives an individual serving.

2 tablespoons butter
½ cup sugar
2 eggs
½ cup self-rising flour
4 tablespoons jam

- Beat butter and sugar until creamy and add well-beaten eggs and flour. Put jam in four well buttered large tea cups and half fill cups with mixture. Place in saucepan in 2 inches of water and steam for 30 minutes. To serve, tip out on each plate. Great with whipped cream or custard.

Makes 4 servings.

GOLDEN PUDDING

4 tablespoons butter
4 tablespoons golden syrup*
¾ cup milk
½ teaspoon baking soda
1 pinch salt
1 cup self-rising flour

• Melt butter in pan and add syrup, milk, baking soda, salt, and the sifted flour. Mix well together. Pour into greased ovenproof bowl and cover with aluminum foil. Place in pan in 2 inches of water, and boil for 2 hours. Check water level often.

Makes 4.

*As we have noted elsewhere (page 162) golden syrup is a popular cooking ingredient in many Australian desserts. Substitutes are difficult. For this recipe you could try using the same quantity of marmalade, since there are quite a few other golden pudding recipes that make this substitution. Our guess is that marmalade is the authentic English version of this popular pudding, and golden syrup is the Australian adaptation.

PINEAPPLE PUDDING

Sauce:
3 tablespoons butter
¼ cup brown sugar
1 can (8 ounces) pineapple rings

- Cream butter and sugar and spread the mixture on the inside of a 9-inch greased ovenproof dish. Drain the pineapple rings and place on top of mixture, cutting rings in half if necessary.

Batter:
6 tablespoons butter
⅓ cup fine sugar
2 eggs
½ cup self-rising flour
1 pinch salt
1 tablespoon warm water
½ teaspoon vanilla

- Cream butter and sugar; add eggs beating well after each addition. Sift flour and salt together and add to mixture along with water and vanilla. Spread batter over top of pineapple. Bake in 375-degree oven for 35 to 40 minutes. Turn pudding upside down on serving dish, so that pineapple sits on top of cake. This dish is delicious served warm with ice cream. If there's any left over (not likely), you can use it the next day as a cake. It cuts nicely into slices. Try it with a nice cup of tea (see cuppa tea, page 225), especially if you drink tea without sugar.

Makes 8 servings.

ABOUT PINEAPPLE: Pineapple was not often found in Australian recipes prior to the 1960s, even though it has been widely cultivated for many decades in Queensland, Australia's tropical northeastern state. Today, pineapple more than any other fruit sets Australian dishes apart from her English cooking heritage. Pineapple is most typical in Australian meat dishes.

MOM'S PINEAPPLE DESSERT

1 can (8 ounces) pineapple chunks
2 eggs, separated
1 teaspoon sugar
2 ¾ cups milk
1 box (4-serving size) raspberry Jell-O

- Drain and reserve juice from pineapple. Cut pineapple small, and place in glass dish. Put the egg yolk, sugar, and milk in a pot and heat until thick, stirring constantly. Pour over pineapple, place in refrigerator, and allow to set. Add enough water to reserved juice to make 1 ½ cups liquid. Heat to almost boiling and add Jell-O. Let set in refrigerator. When almost set, beat egg whites stiffly and fold into Jell-O. Spread over custard and allow to set. Serve with whipped cream.
Serves 4.

HOPE'S SWEET

1 can (14 ounces) unsweetened condensed milk (chilled)
⅓ cup fine sugar
2 teaspoons gelatin
½ cup boiling water
2 tablespoons coffee essence,
or 2 tablespoons coffee cordial,
or pulp of 4 passion fruit

- Pour unsweetened milk into bowl and beat. Add fine sugar. Dissolve gelatin in ½ cup boiling water and add to mixture when cool. Add your choice of coffee or passion fruit. Place in refrigerator and chill. Serve with chocolate mint wafers.
Serves 4 to 6.

ABOUT PASSION FRUIT: see page 216.

ABOUT COFFEE ESSENCE: Coffee essence is virtually unknown in the United States, although it is common in England and Canada. It does turn up in gourmet food stores in America. Coffee essence has a distinctive taste, not especially like coffee as we know it today. It was a special treat for us, as kids, to be allowed to have a cup of coffee essence (one teaspoonful in hot milk) instead of the regulation cup of tea. Coffee essence was always sold mixed with chicory, which is what gave it the different taste.

PEACH TRIFLE

1 can (8 ounces) peaches
sponge cake (page 174)
lemon butter (page 219)
1 ¼ cups custard*
½ teaspoon gelatin
1 egg white
peach slices and nuts for garnish

- Drain peaches and save juice. Spread pieces of sponge with lemon butter. Place sponge cake in dish, top with sliced peaches, and cover with custard. Beat the egg to stiff peak. Dissolve gelatin in ½ cup heated peach juice and when nearly set, beat into egg white. Spoon on top of custard and decorate with peaches and nuts.

VARIATION: Soak pieces of sponge in sherry.

Makes 4 to 6 servings.

Sponge cake is not absolutely necessary for this dish, or any other trifle for that matter. In American cookbooks, trifles are usually presented as the most typical of English desserts. Yet again, we must admit that this dish, while not uniquely Australian, is nevertheless part of the cooking and eating tradition of Australians! One of the reasons trifles are such popular desserts is that Australian mums cook lots of cakes. There is often cake left over, or lost in a multitude of containers kept for storing the many kinds of biscuits and cakes that might be available at any one time in an Australian kitchen, especially at holiday time. Trifles are most often made with such leftovers. We have found that trifles are very popular with our American guests. They are easy to make, yet one rarely finds them in American restaurants.

*Custard is made from custard powder which can be purchased from most gourmet stores or Australian specialty stores (see appendix). Prepared vanilla pudding may be substituted.

PEACH MELBA

This popular Australian dessert is made up in individual glass dishes. For each serving you will need:

1 piece of sponge cake (page 174)
½ large peach (fresh or canned)
peach syrup (from can)
sweet sherry (sprinkling only!)
whipped cream
puréed strawberries and/or raspberries
vanilla ice cream (optional)

- Place the sponge in bottom of glass dish, top with half peach, cut side up. Sprinkle with peach syrup and sweet sherry. (Add scoop of ice cream if desired.) Pipe whipped cream into center of peach. Pour berries over peach and sponge.

ABOUT MELBA: This dessert was named after the great opera singer Dame Nellie Melba, so the story goes. It is popular in restaurants, and appears in many different variations. Dame Nellie Melba was a legend in her own time. Just the sound of her name—a contraction of Melbourne, her birth place—sent people into swoons of adoration. Dame Nellie rose to success at the Royal Covent Garden in London during the golden years, and dominated the international opera scene from the 1890s till well after World War I. In 1914, she played one performance at Covent Garden before no fewer than seven kings and queens. In San Francisco in 1898, her rendition of *The Star Spangled Banner* in the music lesson scene of the *Barber of Seville* to a despondent audience at the height of the Spanish American war, brought the house down. On her international tours, especially to Australia, she was mobbed by screaming crowds in much the same way that rock stars are mobbed today. She accepted this as her due, noting, "There are lots of Duchesses, but only one Melba."

APPLE PANCAKES

½ cup flour
1 pinch salt
1 egg
1 ¼ cups milk
1 to 2 apples
2 tablespoons butter
1 lemon
confectioners' sugar

- Sift flour and salt; break egg into the mound of flour. Using a wooden spoon, gradually stir flour into the egg until it will take no more. Add half the milk gradually, until all flour is absorbed. Beat well until bubbles form. (If batter is well beaten, the pancakes will be lighter.) Stir in the rest of the milk, and allow to stand for 1 hour. Peel and grate apples, fold into mixture. Mixture should be a little thin.

- Place a small piece of butter in the pan, melt, then pour out and wipe out with paper towel. Place another piece of butter in pan, and heat till quite hot. Drop large spoonful of batter into pan and fry until golden brown; turn with wide knife or spatula. When cooked on both sides, remove and place on piece of paper. Sprinkle with confectioners' sugar. These pancakes should be thin and large in size, so that they can be rolled up, and served on a hot plate. Serve with additional sugar plus a slice of lemon. They are delicious with lemon juice and sugar. Whipped cream is a bit of all right, too!

Makes 6 (4-inch) pancakes.

ABOUT PANCAKES: It's hard to imagine how Australia could have anything new to offer America, the land of pancakes. But we have never seen apple pancakes like these in any American restaurant. Apple fritters—slices of apple deep-fried in batter—are common enough, but they are unequal to these cakes.

PIKELETS (DROP SCONES)

These are a variation of pancakes, but are smaller, thicker, and a little heavier than the usual pancake.

½ cup self-rising flour
1 pinch salt
4 tablespoons fine sugar
1 egg
½ to ⅓ cup milk
oil for pan

- Sift flour and salt, add sugar. Drop unbeaten egg into middle of bowl and stir. Add enough milk until the batter is fairly thick. Beat well. Have griddle hot and well oiled (not margarine, use cooking oil). Don't use too much oil, as uneven browning may result. Drop a tablespoonful of the batter onto the griddle (use a tablespoon). Turn once only. Serve on hot plate. Offer a variety of jellies, butter, jam, honey and whipped cream for toppings.

Makes 8 (4-inch) pikelets.

In America, of course, one would naturally use maple syrup. This syrup is not widely available in Australia, because the climate is not conducive to maple trees—there is not enough rain and it is too warm. These days, though, imitation maple syrup is widely available. Traditional Aussies do not eat pancakes for breakfast, as do Americans, and the idea that one might eat these along with syrup *and* bacon or sausage would cause any Aussie to turn up his or her nose! This is strange when one considers that Aussies eat a lot of their main meat dishes with pineapple and other fruits.

Chapter 11

Icings, Fillings, and Spreads

*A*ustralian icing has a different consistency from the frosting most commonly found on American cakes and cookies. It is not as soft, and develops a slightly hard surface when it dries. The closest we have found to it in America is the vanilla frosting on donuts that have sat around on the shelf for most of the day. There is a type of icing used on decorative cakes, such as wedding cakes, which Australians call "plastic icing." This icing is very thick and sweet, often flavored with almond essence. As its name implies, it isn't really meant to be eaten, it is only for decoration.

There are many sauces, but none that one could claim are special to Australia. Lemon spreads and fillings are popular, along with various sauces that are used on Christmas puddings. Brandy cream is one such sauce.

BRANDY CREAM

1 egg, separated
¾ cup fine sugar
½ to 1 cup whipped cream
3 tablespoons brandy

- Beat white of egg until stiff; gradually add sugar. Beat egg yolk slightly and add whipped cream. Fold into egg and sugar mixture. For thicker sauce, add more whipped cream. Pour in brandy slowly. When plum pudding is served piping hot, pour sauce over each serving.

Makes one cup.

VANILLA ICING (FROSTING)

½ cup water
1 cup sugar
1 egg white
1 to 2 drops vanilla

- Boil water and sugar together until a thread forms from a fork dipped into the mixture. Beat the egg white until stiff. Allow sugar mixture to slightly cool, then pour over egg white, add vanilla, and beat until a thick cream forms. Spread over cake.

Makes enough for one cake.

CHOCOLATE ICING

½ cup confectioners' sugar
4 tablespoons grated chocolate,
or 2 tablespoons cocoa
3 tablespoons water

- Sift sugar and place in saucepan with chocolate or cocoa. Add water and stir until warm. Spread over cake.

Makes enough for one cake.

LEMON ICING

1 cup sugar
1 lemon

- Place sugar and juice of lemon in saucepan. Stir until all lumps are gone and thick cream has formed. Spread over cake.

Makes enough for one cake.

PASSION FRUIT SPREAD

Passion fruit is extremely popular in Australia, whether used in spreads, jellies, or in Pavlova (page 196) fillings. They are rarely found in America, although they would thrive in the warm California climate. Passion fruit grows on a vine, which may be cultivated in a manner similar to a grape vine. Their leaves and stems, however, are very different from grape vines. The fruit is about the size and shape of an egg, with a smooth skin and deep brownish purple color, like the color of eggplant. When thoroughly ripe, the skin shrivels and becomes very wrinkled. This is a sign that the inside is sweet and delicious. The fruit inside is a bright yellow pulp containing scores of small black seeds.

Australians eat the seeds as well as the pulp, even though *The Joy of Cooking* doesn't recommend it. One of our moms used to make homemade vanilla ice cream, then cut open a passion fruit and simply pour the pulp on top. But for a real treat, when we became bored with the usual run of sandwich fillings for our school lunches, our mom would prepare sandwiches with passion fruit spread.

3 eggs
4 tablespoons butter
8 passion fruits
2 cups sugar
½ cup lemon juice
½ cup water

- Beat eggs, add rest of ingredients, and mix together. Simmer until thick. Allow to cool, store in refrigerator in closed container up to 3 weeks. Spread thinly on bread and butter sandwiches.

Makes 2 cups.

ABOUT PASSION FRUIT: We used never to see fresh passion fruit in any American shops, until recently. Australia has four indigenous types of passion fruit but the one that is edible was originally imported from South America. We have, on occasion, found cans of passion fruit pulp (available widely in Australia) in our local gourmet food store. These are invariably excellent, even as good as the fresh pulp.

MOCHA FONDUE SAUCE

8 ounces milk chocolate
¾ cup heavy cream
2 tablespoons instant coffee powder
2 tablespoons Tia Maria

- Break chocolate into small pieces. Place into a heavy-based pan with the cream and instant coffee. Stir over gentle heat until chocolate is melted. Add Tia Maria and serve in a heatproof dish. Serve with pieces of fruit, strawberries, banana, or pineapple and cubes of cake. Whipped cream may be served also. Guests dip pieces of fruit into the sauce and eat.

Makes 1 cup.

BETSY'S LEMON FILLING

1 cup sugar
1 cup water
juice of 2 lemons
1 to 2 teaspoons grated lemon rind
2 tablespoons cornstarch
2 tablespoons custard powder (page 154)
1 tablespoon butter

- Boil sugar, water, juice, and rind together. Thicken with cornstarch and custard powder. Add butter when thickened. It will set when cool.

Makes 1 cup.

LEMON BUTTER

1 lemon
4 tablespoons butter
1 cup sugar
2 eggs

- Grate rind from lemon, extract juice. Soften butter, mix with sugar, egg, and rind, adding lemon juice until desired consistency is reached.

Makes 1 cup.

LEMON HONEY

2 lemons
1 cup sugar
4 tablespoons butter
2 eggs

- Grate rind from lemons, extract juice. Place all ingredients in pan and heat until thickens.

Makes 1 cup.

Chapter 12

Drinks and Drinking

*A*ustralia is a society of drinkers, of which there are two classes: tea drinkers and beer drinkers. People may be one or the other, or both, depending on the time of the day and the day of the week. The day is divided according to when one drinks, and what one drinks. Cups of tea help break up the day's work. Glasses of beer help one relax after a day's work, and pass the time on Saturdays. In the old days, there was no beer on Sundays. You had to take home your bottles of beer the night before. These days, pubs are open Sundays, as are many other places, although they are less frequented on this day. Sundays are more for visiting friends and relatives and drinking tea.

There are certain unwritten rules about how to fix drinks (both beer and tea) and how to behave socially when drinking. Drinking beer before lunchtime on a weekday or before about 11:00 a.m. on a Saturday is considered to be a sign of an "alky" (alcoholic). The exception to this rule is when you are on a weekend binge with the mates (perhaps at a footy or on a fishing trip), during which time it might be a sign of drinking strength to have a beer for breakfast. Tea can be taken at any hour.

Beer and tea are enjoyed especially at spectator sports, such as Aussie Rules Football (footy) and cricket. Actually, cricket would be dead without either. One game of cricket takes five days to finish (though it could be less). It's probably the most boring game in the world (after baseball). The highlights are the breaks for tea every afternoon, and the strange names for field positions (such as "silly mid on," "slips," and "square leg"). No wonder the spectators take to playing cards and drinking large quantities of beer to fill in the time between each moment of excitement when a batsman is bowled out or hits a six (a home run).

The situation with footy is a little different. This game, played in the Australian winter in the southern states is very exciting. (The coldest it gets is in the low 40s.) It is played on a huge oval-shaped field, about twice the size of an American football field, with 18 players on each side. Many spectators take along their flask of tea to sip and keep warm. Although many stadiums now have a lot of seating, the vision we have of Aussie Rules games as spectators is of thousands of fans standing for the entire game (about 1 hour not counting time out) just as they would probably stand in the bar after the game. Beer helps to lubricate the voices of the barrackers (spectators who yell), many of whom spend much time heaping abuse on the umpire (referee). When there is a lot of beer, blues (brawls) break out among the yahoos (rowdy hooligans) and drongoes ("bloody no-hopers"). Things got so bad over the years, that most footy stadiums now will not allow spectators to bring their own beer into the stadium (they used to bring in car fridges full of them). Now, one can only buy beer at the stadium, and never in bottles. This is because the hurled bottles hurt the players and umpire. There are also non-drinking sections of the stadium.

Soda is just as popular as in America. But if you ask for a soda in a milk bar (see below) you will not be understood, or you will be given soda water and thought of as weird. You have to ask for a "soft drink" or ask for a specific flavor. There is a wider range of soda flavors available in Australia than in the U.S., including some that are hardly known in America, such as passion fruit. (We have noticed, however, that certain exotic flavors have begun to appear in certain fruit juices and iced teas). Aussie kids drink a lot of "cordial" which is a sweet, non-carbonated drink that is mixed up from a concentrate and tastes something like Gatorade. Flavors available are usually various citrus and tropical fruits.

Also popular is a powder usually called "lemon saline" that most moms keep in their kitchens. This tastes similar to some popular brands of digestive carbonated ("fizzy") drinks, such as Brioschi, but with a stronger lemon flavor. Saline is thought to be a very good thirst quencher.

Two other "cordials" (these are not alcoholic and are nothing like American cordials, which are called *liqueurs* in Australia) are worthy of mention. These are lemon squash and lime juice cordial. One occasionally sees these at an American gourmet food store, and even in a regular supermarket. A little lime juice cordial mixed with cold soda water is a wonderful thirst quencher on a hot day, of which Australia has many. Lemon squash cordial is mixed with soda water to make a drink called lemon squash. One buys these mainly in a bar. They are almost acceptable in lieu of drinking beer (almost).

Many countries have distinctive settings where people traditionally meet to drink a little and talk. Australia has two such abodes. A pub is the most widely established place to go if you wish to speak with "the locals" and drink beer. If you want to drink anything else, you are probably better off not going to a bar, although we have noticed that things are changing rapidly. Some bars (usually in clubs or upscale pubs) even offer cappuccino. One is constantly amazed at the number of pubs in every Australian town. There is certainly no shortage of them. Pubs are essentially meeting places to talk, joke, sometimes play darts or snooker, but certainly never for business. (You might be able to place a few bets on the horses as well.)

Another Australian institution is the milk bar. These little corner stores are everywhere in the suburbs and towns. If you like milk drinks, especially milk shakes, then these are the places to go. You will have to stand up, though, while you drink your milk shake. Milk bars tend to be very small, and have no space for seating. Kids go to them mostly, usually on errands for Mom to buy a few small cooking items like butter or sugar; or to buy some lollies (candy) with small change.

Drinking Tea

In contrast to beer drinking, tea drinking has not, until very recently, taken place in public places. Tea rooms are in ample supply in England (as are pubs), where one can get a good cup of tea, and a scone or biscuit. There have never been as many tea rooms in Australia as in England, and many of those that existed have become coffee shops that boast cappuccino and espresso coffee. But that is another story, and another cookbook! Our guess is that the tea room did not flourish in Australia for the simple reason that people of our parents' generation did not trust others to make a good cup of tea. Tea was a drink made only at home. Only there could one be sure that it would be made according to one's taste. So, how *do* you make a good cuppa?

CUPPA TEA (CUP OF TEA)

Items and ingredients required are:
Medium sized teapot (preferably china)
tea cozy
sugar to taste
English breakfast tea
boiling water
tea cups and saucers
teaspoons
whole milk to taste
tea strainer (optional)

- Boil water using any method. Pour a little boiling water into tea pot and swirl around so that the teapot becomes warm. This is very important (not sure why, but it is).

- Measure out the amount of tea you will need. One level teaspoon per cup is the usual guide, then add "one for the pot."

- Immediately pour the rapidly boiling water into the pot. Replace lid, cover with a tea cozy to keep it warm. A tea cozy is usually a knitted thing that slips over the tea pot like a ski mask. It is often an ancient family heirloom that some distant aunt knitted. Do not place teapot over heat at this stage (or any stage for that matter), or bring to boil. This will ruin the taste of the tea (makes it taste like dish water).

- The tea must now be left to "draw" for awhile. This will normally take about 5 minutes or more. Some hasten this process by lifting the teapot and gently tilting it back and forth. It's better simply to wait. There are other things to do, anyway.

- While the tea is drawing, ask your tea drinkers how they take their tea. In Australia, responding to this question that you will have yours black with lemon, may be tolerated, but it would not be well taken. Only on special occasions do Aussies drink their tea with lemon. People do drink tea black, but most drink it white.

- Now we come to the sticky part. It is rumored that the Queen (of England, of course) adds the milk to her tea last. The established practice in Australia is the opposite. The milk must be placed in the cup first. The tea tastes much better this way. You do have to be more adept at guessing the amount of milk to pour in the cup, especially as you can rarely be sure how strong the tea will be when it is poured. A rule of thumb is to pour about half an inch of milk into the cup. While it would be best if you didn't, it's O.K. to ask a guest whether the tea is strong enough, and to add either tea, milk, or more hot water, to adjust to the desired strength.

- Having resolved this problem to your satisfaction, place the strainer on the cup and pour the tea through it. Always pour the tea in the kitchen, then take the cup to your guest. *Never* allow any tea to splash into the saucer. (This seems a bit silly, since surely this is exactly what the saucer is for!) An alternative method is to pass around the cups, then bring the teapot and small pitcher of milk around, and allow guests to pour their own. In this case, though, one must have a silver tea service—an ornate silver teapot with a small silver milk jug covered with a doily with little beads sewn into its edge.

- Depending on how strong the tea pours, fill the cup to about 5/8 inch from the top. If the tea strength seems all right (it should be a soft tan color), top the cup up to about 1/8 inch from the top with boiling water.

- Tea drinkers always add their own sugar if they wish.

- A tea strainer is certainly desirable, because it makes drinking the last half inch of the tea from the cup much easier. However, there is no special rule about this. If you do not use a strainer, and your guest takes a second cup of tea, always empty out the dregs of tea leaves from the cup before refilling.

- After you have poured the first cups of tea, refill the teapot with more boiling water, and allow it to draw once again, while you drink your first cups.

DON'T use fancy teas, rose tea, mint tea, Chinese tea, or whatever. They may be fine for other purposes, but for making a true blue Aussie cuppa, there's no place for them here.

Beer and Beer Drinking

Making "home brew" is as popular in Australia as it is in England and America. The recipes are much the same, so we will not reproduce them here. However, with a little knowledge of the drinking customs of Aussies, one may approximate certain beer-related drinks using ingredients available in the United States.

Australian beers, and beers from just about everywhere can be bought from most American beverage stores these days. Fosters is the most widely distributed Australian beer in America. One can find those huge cans of Fosters and regular-sized bottles in most places. Coopers beer (from southern Australia) is also available from time to time. This beer is the closest one can get to a commercialized home brew. It has a sediment in the bottom (it's supposed to), so you need to leave the bottle sit for a day or so before you drink it. And when you pour, pour slowly so that air does not bubble back into the bottle and disturb the sediment. Leave about the last ¼ inch of sediment in the bottle. This beer is truly delicious to the beer connoisseur.

We have not often seen any Australian stout in American stores(Coopers makes some that looks like soup). However, the classic Irish stout, Guinness is available everywhere.

While stout and beer are great on their own, one can make popular Australian drinks by mixing them.

Mother-in Law. In a 7-ounce glass, pour stout up to within 1 ½ inches of the rim. Top up with a bitter beer, (that is not an ale or lager, but a beer—Canada makes lots of these.) How did this drink earn its name? The drink is "stout and bloody bitter."

Half-and Half. Make the same as the Mother-in-Law, but half stout and half bitter. You might use half lite beer and half regular beer.

Shandy. If you ask for a lemonade in Australia, you will be given a soda that looks and tastes very much like Seven-Up. A Shandy is made by pouring beer to within ½ inch of the top of the glass, then topping up with lemonade. Children are commonly allowed to drink a light shandy (lemonade with a dash of beer) on special occasions. Try it. Some like it, some hate it.

Beer Glasses

Depending on the Australian state, the names of beer glasses may vary, according to shape and size. In Victoria, one may buy a "glass of beer" which is a regulation 7-ounce glass. These glasses used to be tapered from top to bottom, with a heavy base. Many different shapes have now appeared. A larger sized 10-ounce glass called a "pot" is available for those who would like to be thought of as big drinkers. If you can stand the "rubbishing" (kidding, jokes made about your personal adequacy) from your mates, you might ask for a "pony" which is a small 5-ounce glass.

By the way, Aussies have quite a disarming sense of humor which can catch Americans unaware. The favorite pastime is to kid or rubbish mates (not usually done to strangers, unless there's good reason for it). This can amount to quite personal remarks about how one does just about everything (or how one can't do things), and appears to the outsider as insulting and uncouth. The extent to which one can take this good-natured ribbing shows how good a "bloke" (genuine fellow) one is.

In a bar, Australians will also spin yarns (tell tall tales), especially to unsuspecting visitors from another country. Again, this is part of the Aussie sense of humor, and should not be taken personally. Aussies are great kidders!

In other parts of Australia, the names of beer glasses may be different again. For example, in New South Wales, the usual size glass is called a "middie" (10 ounces) and the larger size is called a "schooner."

We relate all of this because Aussies take their beer drinking very seriously, as they do their tea drinking. Beer must be poured just right, and in the right glass. There was an outcry quite some years now when health regulations were introduced requiring that fresh clean glasses be provided each time the customer in a bar ordered a beer. This regulation cut across the time honored and much studied practice of always using the same glass for a refill.

The reason for the outcry was that an experienced beer drinker can tell one glass of beer from another, even though to the uninitiated they may look the same. A fresh glass usually does not retain the head (white froth at the top) as well as a used glass. This is extremely important for Aussie beer drinkers. If you pour them a glass of beer that has no head, it will be returned to you with a comment like, "I don't drink dog's...." Or, "What do yer think I am, a bloody Pom (Englishman)?"

It takes practice to pour a glass of beer with just the right amount of head (froth). In Victoria, a quarter inch of froth is considered right. The opposite is also unacceptable: too much froth. If you serve a beer with a lot of froth, an Aussie might remark, "Well, yer gonna put a bow-tie on it, mate?" An Australian will also have experimented with different detergents, to find out which ones produce the best beer glasses. Many wash their beer glasses separately from other dishes without any detergent at all, because it is thought that detergent ruins the head-keeping capabilities of the glass. Many hours may be passed in a bar discussing the science of beer pouring.

Drinking Beer—Aussie Style

Unless you visit Australia, you will not have to be concerned with some of the hints provided in this section. But it might be fun to have an Aussie night with your friends, if you have any who like beer drinking.

The most important thing to know is how to behave in an Aussie bar. Here are a few hints.

- If you are female, it's probably best not to go into a public bar in an Aussie pub. There's no law against it (though there used to be!), but not many do. You would be best advised to find the "ladies lounge" or "Saloon Bar" where the surroundings and clientele would be more designed for sheilas (girls). Things are changing, of course, and one does find more and more women in a public bar these days. But the bar is still, by and large, a men's haven.

- To soften the shock of entering into a public bar, try the saloon bar first. This is a special part of the bar set aside for those who are prepared to pay a little more for their glass of beer, and enjoy slightly better, and quieter surroundings. It is O.K. to ask for mixed drinks either in this bar, or in the ladies lounge, where it's expected.

- If you are taken to the bar with some newly found Aussie mates, beware! We have known a number of Americans who visited Australia on business, and after the working day they were spirited off to the pub to "have a few." A great Aussie pastime is to initiate foreigners into Aussie beer drinking. The rate of drinking is usually much faster than the innocent visitor is accustomed to, and the beer tends to pack a bigger kick.

- If you find yourself in a "drinking school" (a group of three or more drinkers), then you may be in trouble. Tradition requires that each member of the school "shout" (take his turn in paying for a round of drinks). Anyone who pulls out in the middle of a round, or who doesn't take his turn, is considered to be a bludger (freeloader). Obviously, if the school is large, you're in for quite a time. The only way to extricate oneself from such a situation is to pay for an extra round of drinks before you leave.

- If you are alone, be careful which stool you sit on. Very often there are set places where the local boozers (steady drinkers) always sit. Years ago, when one of us "lived" in a pub, we saw "blues" (rowdy rough brawls) caused by such inconsiderate behavior.

If you are careful to abide by these rules, you can go into any Aussie bar and expect to be treated well. Though they are rowdy places, smoke-filled and smelling of yeast and beer soaked into the very woodwork of the buildings, they are also congenial places, where one can always find a mate to talk to.

The tradition of heavy beer drinking probably dates back to shearing times late in the nineteenth century. The shearers would work constantly until the shearing was done, receiving meals and lodging on the homestead. When the shearing was completed the men would be paid their checks. Many took off to the nearest pub in search of relaxation and excitement. To be "lambed down" was to be led astray by others, or oneself, into spending an entire check on booze:

The shades of night were falling fast,
As down a steep gully passed
A man whom you could plainly see
Had just come off a drunken spree,
Lambed down.
He'd left the station with his check,
And little evil did he reck;
At Ryan's pub he felt all right,
And yet he was, before next night,
Lambed down.
"Oh, stay!" old Ryan said, "and slip
Your blanket off, and have a nip;
I'll cash your check and send you on."

He stopped, and now his money's gone—
Lambed down.
He's got the shakes and thinks he sees
Blue devils lurking in the trees;
Oh, shearers! if you've any sense
Don't be on such pretense
Lambed down.
—"Lambed Down," Anonymous, about 1870.

The reader may wonder why we have devoted so much space to beer drinking. Fact is, alcohol has played an important part in Australia's history. There was a time when rum was the main form of currency in early colonial days. It was dear to the hearts of all Aussies:

Convicts' Rum Song
Cut yer name across me backbone,
Stretch me skin across a drum
Iron me up on Pinchgut Island
From today till Kingdom Come!

I will eat yer Norfolk Dumpling
Like a juicy Spanish plum,
Even dance the Newgate Hornpipe*
If ye'll only give me RUM!
—Anonymous

*Newgate was the famous prison and site of London's scaffold, on which criminals were hanged until they were dead. In the process of strangulation, the body twisted and was said to "dance."

Chapter 13

Outback Cooking

*A*merica has her Wild West. Australia has her outback.
Many of Australia's most moving novels are set in the
outback. There lies the mystery and romance of Australia. The
outback is enormous, about four fifths of the country's area.
There is also a lot of bush land in the high plains surrounding
the coastal areas, populated by more wild life. In the northeast, where the climate is tropical, there is abundant wild life
and vegetation. With such a varied climate, there is a wide
range of plants and animals, many of which are edible. Australia's Aborigines lived off this land for many centuries. Only recently have Australians begun to learn about and experiment
with such uniquely Australian foods.

In the first edition of this book we included very few Australian
indigenous foods. One would have thought that, stuck in the
isolation of the outback, one would have to "live off the land."
But the fact is that Australia's early settlers brought their traditional foods with them—flour, tea, beef, lamb (and rabbits!)—the
traditional foods of their Anglo-Saxon culture. But traditional
outback cooking is more a method—even an attitude—that draws
on the romance of the outback wilderness, that emphasizes the
primitive use of the campfire as the vehicle of cooking anything.
So in the first edition we included a few classic dishes and

methods of cooking that are fun to do. These are reproduced in this chapter and are identified as "outback."

We are also presenting recipes that could not be easily reproduced in the Australian outback without the help of gourmet food stores and a modern kitchen. In recent years there has been a strong movement in Australia to find a cuisine that is "uniquely Australian," which is to say a cuisine that uses ingredients of Australia's indigenous flora and fauna. Some of these ingredients one might find by foraging in the forests, but most of them could only be found by an expert in such matters. They can more likely be found in gourmet food stores or Australian souvenir shops. One may experience them in a restaurant that serves "modern Australian" cuisine, although this type of cooking usually also includes the many adaptations of Asian and other imported cultural influences on Australian cooking of the past 20 years or so. Where possible, we have recommended American substitutions. The hunters among our readers will have the greatest success in finding these alternatives.

Outback Cooking

There is greater opportunity to try out bush cooking in many parts of the United States than in Australia because the danger of forest fires is less (depending, of course, on where one lives in the States). If you do try some outback cooking, please, please use fire safety precautions. Don't have a large fire, just a very small one is needed for most cooking, and clear the ground for 10 feet around. Preferably, use the safest type of cooking fire, a trench fire. All one needs is a small trench dug in the ground, with the fire lit in the trench. In most of Australia during the summer months, it would be extremely unlikely that one could light a cooking fire in the bush, due to the danger of fire (and there are severe punishments for doing so). Most Aussies, during these months, if they do want to cook outdoors, will use a portable gas barbecue. But there are many days of extreme fire danger when even gas barbecues cannot be used. In public parks, electric barbecues are provided, and are often free.

The best time to cook in the Australian bush is in the late winter or early spring. The smell of eucalyptus just after a rain is hard to beat. Better, we think, than the smell of a pine forest, though this is a little bit like comparing rubies and diamonds. By the way, Australians call eucalyptus trees "gum trees." There are about 1,000 varieties, of which the famed koala eats only one.

Killing and Eating Australian wildlife

Killing animals in order to eat, if one is actually dependent on the land for survival, surely seems reasonable. But we doubt that there is anyone who actually does this in Australia today, including the Australian Aborigines, although we are told that there are a few in the far northern part of Australia who continue to try to cling to the old ways. We have included some recipes that require that you have in hand a dead animal or two. Frankly, they're included for the sake of curiosity. We wouldn't want to see a single hair (or scale) of any Australian animal harmed. And we're sure just about every Australian thinks the same way.

However, in recent years the farming of certain species has become popular, so that their meat is now available in upscale restaurants under the guise of exotic-sounding dishes. There are now farms for emu (the large flightless bird similar to the ostrich), crocodiles, camels (imported to help in transportation on Australia's desert), buffalo (water buffalo, a different species from the American buffalo), and kangaroo. In some parts of Australia where kangaroo are abundant, it is permitted to hunt them (only certain species). Many sea creatures are also farmed such as oysters, barramundi, and even yabbies (freshwater crayfish or lobster).

ROAST TASMANIAN HEN (modern)

This recipe is unique in its use of vine leaves. Grapes were introduced into Australia from California. The Tasmanian hen, locally called "bantam," is very popular. There are other hens or fowl, such as the mallee fowl, scrub hen, bush turkey (about the size of a small hen), and the Australian water hen. Americans may substitute quail or Cornish game hen.

Tasmanian hens, quail, or Cornish hen
1 slice bacon per bird
grape vine leaves
2 tablespoons melted butter
day-old bread squares
oil for frying
red currant jelly
gravy
dried bread crumbs

* Truss each hen and brush with melted butter. Place vine leaf on the breast and bacon slice on leaf. Secure with strong toothpick or skewer. Cover lightly with aluminum foil and roast for 30 minutes at 400 degrees. Baste frequently. To fry bread, heat oil to a very hot temperature (as for French fries) and drop in squares of day-old bread. Quickly brown and remove so that it remains crisp. Serve hen on fried bread spread with red currant jelly. Top with brown gravy sprinkled with dried bread crumbs.

4 servings per hen

WALLABY STEW (modern)

Wallabies are small kangaroos. As with rabbit, wallaby and kangaroo meat is very lean.

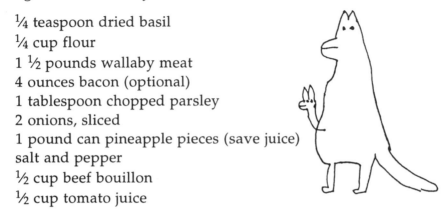

¼ teaspoon dried basil
¼ cup flour
1 ½ pounds wallaby meat
4 ounces bacon (optional)
1 tablespoon chopped parsley
2 onions, sliced
1 pound can pineapple pieces (save juice)
salt and pepper
½ cup beef bouillon
½ cup tomato juice

- If bacon is used, make it is as lean as possible. Mix basil with flour. Cut meat into 1-inch pieces and roll in flour and basil. Place half of meat in bottom of well-greased casserole dish and cover with half of the bacon, parsley, onion, and pineapple pieces. Add salt and pepper to taste. Repeat layers until no ingredients are left. Combine ¼ cup of pineapple juice, bouillon, and tomato juice and pour over casserole. Bake, covered, for about 2 hours at 350 degrees.

Serves 6.

Wallaby is a small species of kangaroo. American substitution for wallaby could be possum or squirrel. There are also possums in Australia, but we don't know of any tradition of eating them.

The wallaby has a special place in the hearts of all Aussies, perhaps because in olden days, kangaroos and wallabies were the guarantee to the poor that there was always a meal there, waiting to be caught, even in the most trying times, as expressed in the following ballad:

Stir the Wallaby Stew

Poor Dad he got five years or more as everybody knows,
And now he lives in Maitland Jail with broad arrows on his
    clothes,
He branded all of Brown's clean-skins and never left a tail,
So I'll relate the family's woes since Dad got put in jail.

Chorus:
So stir the wallaby stew,
Make soup of the kangaroo tail,
I tell you things is pretty tough
Since Dad got put in jail.

They let Dad out before his time, to give us a surprise.
He came and slowly looked around and gently blessed our
    eyes,
He shook hands with the shearer cove and said he thought
    things stale,
So left things here to shepherd us and battled back
to jail.
—*Anonymous*, mid 1800s

PAN-FRIED KANGAROO STEAK IN PORT WINE SAUCE (modern)

2 pounds kangaroo steak, best cut
salt and pepper
4 tablespoons butter or margarine

Port wine sauce:
Grated rind and juice of 3 small oranges
½ cup of water
2 tablespoons margarine
3 tablespoons cornstarch
2 tablespoons sugar
Freshly ground black pepper
¼ cup port wine

- Cut steak into thin slices. Sprinkle with salt and black pepper. Fry in butter until a rich brown on both sides. Remove from pan. Simmer orange rind in water for 5 minutes, strain and add liquid to juice of oranges. Make up to 1 cup with extra water, if necessary. Add margarine to pan and heat, stirring in cornstarch (about 2 minutes). Gradually blend in orange liquid and cook slowly until thickened. Return kangaroo steak to pan and add sugar, pepper and port. Simmer for 2 minutes or until tender. Adjust amount of liquid by adding water or port to taste.

Serves 6.

This recipe is for the large "buck" kangaroos that grow to 15 feet tall, sometimes even taller. Although Australians are great beer drinkers, they also like their drop of port. A bottle of port is often kept on the mantle piece above the fireplace to keep it a little warm. After a day's hunt and a hearty meal, the men gather around the fireplace and sip port. American substitution for kangaroo steak is young venison.

ROAST WILD AUSTRALIAN PIG WITH MINTED APRICOTS (modern)

Care must be taken in preparation of this game animal. Make sure that it is well cooked. American substitution is peccary.

1 wild pig, carefully cleaned and washed
½ lemon
3 ounces cottage cheese
4 tablespoons finely chopped mint
salt and pepper
1 medium can apricot halves, drained
maraschino cherries (optional)

- Preheat oven to 400 degrees. Rub pig with lemon half and place in roasting pan. Allow 35 minutes per pound, plus an additional 35 minutes for cooking time.

- Combine cottage cheese, mint, and salt and pepper to taste. Fill apricot halves. Place in shallow pan and bake in oven 15 minutes before serving. For special effect, decorate pig by attaching apricot halves to outside of pig with toothpick. An occasional maraschino cherry will add to the visual effect.

VARIATION: If you have a rotisserie attachment for your barbecue, roast pig in this fashion, basting with mixture of lemon juice and liquid from apricots.

Each pound serves 4.

ROAST WILD DUCK, VICTORIAN STYLE
(modern)

3 medium onions, chopped
1 tablespoon finely chopped sage
½ cup bread crumbs
2 tablespoons butter, melted
1 egg
salt and pepper to taste
1 wild duck

- Mix first six ingredients to make stuffing. Prepare and truss duck as for any game bird. Stuff body with sage/onion stuffing. Roast at 400 degrees for about 1 ½ hours or more, according to age of the bird. Serve with roast tomatoes, baked apples, and roast potatoes.

1 duck serves 6.

ABOUT AUSTRALIAN DUCKS. The Australian gray or black duck is hunted in most of Australia where there is sufficient habitat. The gray duck is sometimes referred to by Australian hunters as "supercilious" (and no doubt other terms are used in times of frustration) because of a curved black line about the eye that looks like an eyebrow and gives the duck a "so you think you're smart" expression. This recipe originated from Australia's southeastern state of Victoria.

TROUT WITH MACADAMIA NUTS (modern)

4 trout, gutted, cleaned, heads on
flour for coating
freshly ground black pepper
2 to 4 tablespoons butter, for frying
juice of 1 lemon
2 ounces macadamia nuts, coarsely chopped (½ cup)
whole macadamia nuts for garnish
parsley sprigs for garnish
lemon for garnish

- Coat fish with flour and pepper. Melt butter in pan. Add nuts and fry gently for 2 minutes. Be careful not to burn butter. Remove nuts from pan and drain on paper towel. Wipe out pan and add another knob of butter. When melted, add trout and cook gently for 5 to 8 minutes per side. Turn only once, and add squeeze of lemon juice each turn. Test for doneness; flesh should flake easily. Place fish carefully on hot platter, and sprinkle with nuts. Garnish with a few whole macadamia nuts, sprigs of parsley, and thin slices of lemon.

Serves 4.

Trout are found in many of Australia's inland streams. Macadamia nuts were first cultivated as a commercial crop in Queensland, Australia's northeastern tropical state. Only recently have these nuts become popular and they are now grown and processed in Hawaii.

MURRAY ROLL (modern)

2 tablespoons butter or margarine
⅓ to ½ cup flour
½ cup milk
½ cup water (use water from cooked peas)
½ cup cooked peas
1 tablespoon chopped fresh parsley
pastry*
4 large Murray cod fillets
flour
salt and pepper

- Melt butter in pan. Gradually add flour, stirring until smooth. Add milk and water, and stir over medium heat until boiling. Simmer lightly for another 5 to 7 minutes. Sauce should be quite thick. Roll out pastry as thin as possible, but thick enough to fold without breaking. Cut into 4 squares. Roll fish in flour, and sprinkle with salt and pepper to taste. Place 1 fish fillet on each square and cover with white sauce and peas. Sprinkle with parsley. Fold pastry over fish from both sides and stick together with a middle seam. Paint with egg or milk, and bake in oven at 400 degrees for 30 minutes.
Serves 6.

The Murray cod is a popular fish caught in the Murray River and its tributaries in southeastern Australia. Though the word "cod" suggests an ocean fish, the Murray cod is very much a freshwater species. It may grow to 20 pounds or more in large waterways and streams. American substitution: any game fish that grows to sufficiently large size to yield nice-size fillets.

*Any ready-made pastry will do. Puff pastry is sometimes used, though depending on the herbs used, puff pastry may make this dish a little too rich.

TASMANIAN DEVILED RISSOLES
(MEATBALLS) IN CIDER (modern)

½ pound game meat (kangaroo, emu), ground
2 tablespoons cooking oil
1 teaspoon basil
2 tablespoons finely chopped parsley
1 egg
4 tablespoons bread crumbs
⅓ cup beef bouillon or 1 tablespoon port wine in ⅓ cup water
6 tablespoons flour
salt and pepper to taste
1 onion, peeled and sliced into rings
2 celery stalks, chopped
2 carrots, chopped
1 cup dry apple cider (alcoholic, of course)
½ cup beef bouillon
3 tablespoons freshly chopped parsley, for garnish

- Lightly brown ground meat in cooking oil over high heat. Reduce heat, add basil, parsley, egg, and bread crumbs, stirring in bouillon (or port mixture) until correct thickness is obtained. Remove from pan and allow to cool. Take large tablespoons of the meat mixture, form into patties, and roll in 4 tablespoons flour, salt, and pepper.

- Lightly brown rissoles on all sides, then remove from pan. Place vegetables in pan and fry gently until light in color. Add 2 tablespoons flour, stirring as you cook for 1 to 2 minutes. Pour in cider and ½ cup bouillon, stir well, and bring to boil. Lower heat, add rissoles and salt and pepper. Cover and cook for 30 minutes, stirring occasionally. Serve with parsley sprinkled on top.

Serves 4.

It is widely believed that certain notorious "bush rangers" (outlaws) who escaped from the convict settlement in Tasmania early in the eighteenth century either ate or were eaten by the mysterious and frightening Tasmanian devil. The devil is now rarely seen and almost extinct. This recipe has survived with less-exciting game meat, especially those cuts that may be a little tough. In Australia, substitutions may be kangaroo, dingo (a type of wild dog common in northern Australia), wild pig, or maybe wombat (a large, slow nocturnal animal that's too easy to shoot—any good sport wouldn't do it). This recipe also uses apple cider—Tasmania, Australia's island state off the southeastern coast is known as "The Apple Isle." American substitutions are bear or venison meat, which would be excellent.

GALAH SALAD (modern)

2 pounds galah meat*
4 cups long-grain rice
½ cup French dressing
6 tablespoons butter or margarine
2 onions, chopped
4 ounces mushrooms, sliced (1 cup)
1 cup cooked peas
1 can (8 ounces) whole-kernel corn
½ pound cooked shrimp
½ red pepper, chopped
½ green pepper, chopped
4 tablespoons finely chopped parsley
4 ounces ham, chopped

- Steam galahs until tender. Birds can be boiled or roasted, but the meat will be more tender if steamed. Remove meat from bones, and chop into very small pieces. Cook rice and drain well; mix in French dressing. Melt 2 tablespoons butter (or margarine) in pan and sauté chopped onions until transparent. Remove from pan. Add remaining 4 tablespoons of butter to pan, sauté sliced mushrooms until tender. Mix onion and mushrooms into rice. Mix in cooked peas, drained corn, shrimp, chopped peppers, parsley, chopped ham, and galah pieces. Mix together lightly and refrigerate.

Serves 12.

*ABOUT GALAHS: The galah is a gray cockatoo found in many parts of Australia in large flocks. They wreak havoc on farmers' crops, but in many areas they are protected. The flesh, when cooked is a little tough and turns a dark gray. This doesn't matter in a salad recipe, however, in which the meat is cut up into very small pieces. American substitutions are pigeon or squirrel.

NUGGETS NARDOO (modern)

½ cup (1 stick) butter
¾ cup brown sugar
1 egg
1 cup crushed pineapple
1 cup rolled oats
½ cup nardoo paste*
½ cup flour
1 pinch salt
¼ cup chopped walnuts
1 teaspoon salt

- Cream butter and sugar until light and fluffy, add egg. Drain crushed pineapple well, add fruit to mixture. Stir in remaining ingredients until well combined. You may substitute ½ cup flour for the nardoo. Place teaspoonfuls of mixture on ungreased tray. Bake at 375 degrees for 15 to 20 minutes. *Serves 4.*

*ABOUT NARDOO. Nardoo is a plant, native to Australia, found in the outback. It bears edible seeds, from which the Aborigines used to make a paste or dough. We have never met an Australian who has eaten this food, which is surprising because it is supposed to be an intoxicant as well! Nardoo is mentioned in many Australian bush ballads, such as that below which refers to Americans with the fond term (to Australians) of Yankees. No insult is intended to Southerners, but Australians understandably see America as totally north.

No Yankee hide e'er grew outside such beef as we can freeze;
No Yankee pastures make such steers as we send o'er the seas—
As we send o'er the seas, my boys, in shipments every day,
From the far Barcoo, where they eat nardoo, a thousand miles
    away.
—*"A Thousand Miles Away," Anonymous*

BUSH ANGELS (outback)

If you just happen to be trudging through the bush, and just happen to have brought along the following ingredients, you could make these outback desserts and late night snacks when you're telling yarns around the campfire.

slices of bread
can of condensed milk
shredded coconut

- In order to make this bush delicacy, you will need at least 1 grubby (i.e. sticky and dirty) child. Have this chosen kid dip the bread in the sticky condensed milk, a part of bush cooking that only kids could enjoy. Now, cross your fingers, and hope that the bread is not dropped on the bush floor (always dry and dusty). Have your child press the milk-soaked bread in the coconut. Toast over hot coals. Insist that the child hand over the first cooked bush angel to you (if it's clean). These are only for sugar-holics, which means that if you were thinking of sneaking a quick beer before going to bed, forget it.

- Make sure the billy is boiling, and you can sip down a cup of delicious billy tea (page 249) as you munch on your angels. How much closer to heaven could you get? If you take a moment to forget your sticky fingers, you may look up at the huge expanse of the Southern Hemisphere (it looks bigger than the northern sky of course). The sky is always clear, the stars twinkle without fail every night. The Southern Cross is there. Find an Aussie mate to point it out for you.

KANGAROO TAIL SOUP (modern)

1 kangaroo tail (about 3 pounds)
5 cups water
salt and pepper
3 ounces barley
1 onion
1 carrot
½ turnip or small rutabaga
1 stick celery
1 teaspoon chopped parsley

- Wash the tail, trim off fat, divide at joints. Remove meat from bones and cut into small pieces. In a large pan, place bones, meat, water,salt and pepper, and barley and bring slowly to the boil. Skim off fat just before and after boiling.
- Prepare vegetables, dicing small. Add to the soup after it boils and simmer for 2 ½ hours. Remove bones, add additional salt and pepper to taste. Skim off fat if necessary, add parsley. Serve with crisp croutons. Aussies will take it with hot buttered toast.

Serves 6.

Please don't visit Australia with the hope of shooting a kangaroo, not to mention eating it! It is true that in certain parts of Australia, the northern arid areas, kangaroos are thought of as pests by some farmers. This is because they compete with farmers' cattle and sheep for that great scarcity in the Australian outback: life-sustaining grass. Kangaroos are especially a nuisance because they tend to eat the grass down and into the roots, thus destroying the plant, making it difficult to regenerate. In these areas, so we are told, kangaroos are not a protected species, although particular species (such as the Big Red) are protected and endangered.

In our hometown there are many kangaroos in the surrounding bush. They come down to feed on the golf course, which is a convenient source of rich green grass. It is sometimes necessary to shoo them out of the way so one can tee off or putt. While they are tame enough, they will not let one touch them, which is probably pretty smart. We have often wondered whether they laughed at our golf swing as they watched, nonchalantly chewing their breakfast.

ROAST RABBIT (outback)

3 slices bacon
4 tablespoons flour
salt and pepper
2 tablespoons vegetable oil

Stuffing:
½ cup bread crumbs
1 tablespoon chopped parsley
grated rind of 1 lemon
½ teaspoon salt
¼ teaspoon pepper
pinch of nutmeg
1 teaspoon butter, melted
¼ cup milk

- Soak and wash rabbit, as per instructions page xx. Mix all stuffing ingredients together, insert in rabbit, and sew up. Rub with flour seasoned with salt and pepper, and lay bacon slices on top. Fatty bacon is better in this case, as rabbit flesh is very lean. Place in baking pan with vegetable oil, cover lightly with aluminum foil, and bake 1 ½ to 2 hours at 400 degrees. Baste every 15 minutes. Australians do not, as a rule, use cranberry sauce, as the climate is not conducive to the growth of cranberries (not enough water and not cold enough). However, cranberry sauce would be an excellent accompaniment to roast rabbit. Some Australian recipes recommend red or black currant jelly.

Serves 4.

MORE ABOUT RABBITS: Rabbits are not indigenous to Australia, so they are fair game. If you are stuck in the bush without any food (heaven knows how you would get into such a predicament), a rabbit might just save your skin. They're difficult to catch, though, unless you can use some of the (cruel) methods described on page xx. If you're lucky, they can also be easy to catch. Once when walking in the bush our dad pointed out a knee-high tuft of thick grass. These were, he said, favorite sitting spots for rabbits. Suddenly he stopped, and put his finger to his mouth. He was poised over a big tuft of grass. He gave a loud clap, and a rabbit flew out from under us at lightening speed. This rabbit was duly caught and eaten.

ROAST QUAIL (modern)

1 quail
grape vine leaves
1 slice of bacon per quail
2 tablespoons melted butter
fried bread
red currant jelly
gravy
dried bread crumbs

- To clean and pluck quail, see below. Truss quail and brush with melted butter. Place a vine leaf on the breast and on top of this, a bacon slice. Secure with a strong toothpick or skewer. Cover lightly with aluminum foil and roast 1 hour at 400 degrees. Baste frequently. To fry bread, heat oil to very hot, as for French fries; drop in squares of day-old bread. Quickly brown and remove, so that it remains crisp. Serve quail on fried bread, spread with red currant jelly. Top with gravy sprinkled with dried bread crumbs.

1 to 2 quails per serving.

Quail are found in most parts of Australia where they nest in long dry grass. They are a tiny fat bird (a relative of the grouse). Their flocking together when disturbed is remarkable.

TO PREPARE QUAIL: Do not scald bird, as the skin will break. Pluck feathers from one side, holding bird by leg, then by wing. If feathers are difficult to remove, pour boiling water over difficult part. Cut head off, place bird on breast and cut slit in back of neck, pull neck out and cut off close to the body. Cut between vent and tail, pull out entrails with fingers. Chop off legs above the knee joint. Rinse out inside of bird.

We know you'll probably never shoot your own quail, but we've included this just to add a little genuine outback flavor. You could substitute Cornish hens.

JUGGED HARE (outback, sort of)

You need a large "jug" or jar in order to prepare this unusual dish. One is not likely to have such an implement in the outback. But you never know, you may just happen on a lonely homestead a couple of days after you catch the hare.

1 young hare
½-inch slice of bacon
1 onion
3 sprigs thyme
salt and pepper
¾ cup flour

- Skin and clean the hare, and hang it head down for 2 days (1 day if it's too bloody hot to sit out in the sun). It would be best to do something to keep the blowies (flies) away from it while hanging. Take a large wide-mouthed stoneware jar. Place hare in jar, cut bacon into small cubes. Add bacon, onion, thyme, salt and pepper. Make a smooth paste with flour and water and add to hare. Add more water until hare is just covered. Cover jar with cloth or aluminum (called al-u-min-ium by Aussies) foil, and place in a saucepan of hot water. Boil for 3 to 4 hours, depending on size and age of hare.

TO SKIN A HARE OR RABBIT: Using a very sharp knife, cut around the neck, and make a small incision under tail. Open hare's mouth as wide as possible, and force fist down gullet, keeping two fingers pushed out front. Retract and extend fingers once or twice to loosen insides. Push hand further into hare's gullet until index finger reaches tail. Force finger through small incision and curl around tail. Pull tail through incision and grip in hand. With other hand, push down strongly on head of rabbit. With a strong flicking movement across the knee, pull hare inside out. Remove entrails. Reverse procedure, then peel off skin beginning around neck, and pulling down to tail.

CROCODILE ON THE BARBIE (modern)

fresh peppercorns, ground and whole
2 (3 ½ ounce) crocodile steaks
2 teaspoons fresh ginger, finely chopped
1 clove garlic, finely chopped
2 teaspoons macadamia oil
3 ounces bunya nuts
3 teaspoons wattle
2 tablespoons chicken stock
2 tablespoons dry white wine
10 tablespoons cream
chives for garnish

- Grind half the peppercorns, amount to taste. Coat crocodile steaks with peppercorns, garlic, and ginger, seal in plastic wrap or other container, and leave overnight in refrigerator. Cook on barbie at medium heat, turning 2 or 3 times during cooking. In a hot pan, heat oil and lightly fry the bunya nuts until brown, then add wattle, stock, wine, and cream and simmer until thickened. Serve sauce over crocodile, and garnish with chives.

Serves 2 to 4.

ABOUT BUNYA NUTS: These are large seeds from Australia's native pine tree which grows in northern New South Wales and southern Queensland. Regular pine nuts available in most stores could be substituted.

ABOUT WATTLE:. There are over 1,000 species of wattle plants in Australia. These beautiful plants, some which are the size of shrubs, others large trees, produce clumps of small bright yellow flowers in spring (October). Wattle essence is obtained from one of these species, and is now available in most Australian food stores. It is very unlikely that one could find it anywhere in the United States. Substitute either oregano or bay leaves.

DAMPER (outback)

flour
water
butter
jellies and jams
honey
salt
a green stick

- Damper is a traditional scone-like bread baked over or on the campfire. The trick is as much in the cooking as it is in the mixing.

- Prepare a cooking fire by allowing a campfire to burn down to a heap of red coals. Select a green stick, about 3 feet long, that is straight and about 1 inch thick. Try to get one that doesn't require chopping down a whole tree.

- Place flour and salt in mixing bowl, add water a little at a time until a thick dough is formed. Keep the dough as stiff as possible. Knead well and allow to sit for an hour or so. Roll into a long sausage shape, then twist around the green stick so it resembles the doctor's emblem of a serpent on a staff.

- Place stick with damper over fire. The easiest way to cook this damper is to rest the stick on one or two forked sticks, so you don't have to hold it all the time. Turn the damper over every now and again. The most important thing is not to cook the damper too quickly. It may take an hour or more.

- When cooked, remove from fire and break damper from stick. Serve pieces smothered with butter, jam, jellies, or honey. Though it's not Australian, try some maple syrup as well.

(See variation on next page.)

VARIATION (BLACK JELLY BEAN DAMPER): Prepare damper dough as above. Knead into a flat disk, then sprinkle with black jelly beans. Roll up into a ball and place at side of fire, and allow to cook slowly in the embers. If the fire is slow enough, you can leave the damper to cook for 1 to 2 hours. Dough may be also wrapped in aluminum foil. Use any other flavor jelly bean, of course.

VARIATION: Enclose an egg inside the dough. It will be nicely cooked when you retrieve the damper.

BILLY TEA (outback)

Many of the rules of tea making described on page 225 apply to making billy tea. However there are a few differences.

First, you must have a "billy." This is a large can-like metal container with a wire handle attached to the top. This is not very functional because when the billy is boiling, it's very hard to pick up—the wire handle hangs down close to the fire, and against the hot side of the billy. It takes a little practice to thread a strong stick, or your hunting knife under the handle so you can lift the billy off without burning your fingers.

- Prepare a hot, but small fire. Place the billy ¾ full of water on the flames. A black soot coated billy is best, as it heats more quickly. (How you carry it with your other things without getting black all over you is your problem).

- When the water is boiling, remove the billy from the fire as quickly as possible, and immediately add about 6 teaspoons of tea (English Breakfast tea—nothing fancy), depending on the size of the billy. Usually, allow 1 teaspoon for each cup of tea to be made.

- Do not return the billy to the fire. Leave to the side to keep hot, but do not allow to boil. If the tea boils it will taste like bitter soup. Now is the time for the tea to "draw." It is best left to sit for a few minutes. There are various beliefs about how the drawing process may be speeded up. Some advise taking the billy by the handle and swinging it forcefully and evenly round and round over one's head. This does seem to work. However, we have also seen the billy fly away from the handle several times when swung over the head. A gentler way is to tap all around the sides of the billy with a teaspoon.

- Pour tea as directed in Cuppa Tea, page 225. Milk should be added first. When drinking tea in the outback, one never drinks from a cup and saucer. An enamel mug is the traditional container, though not our choice, because it conducts the heat so fiercely that one can burn one's lips very easily.

BUSH VARIATION: Some hardy outback types claim to drink billy tea flavored with a gum leaf (leaf from a eucalyptus tree). If you decide to try this, choose a sweet smelling tree, and break only a tiny piece of leaf (½ inch at the most) into the tea while it is drawing. It is best to drink eucalyptus tea without milk.

ABOUT EUCALYPTUS: It is widely believed that eucalyptus trees have medicinal value. Eucalyptus oil is sold everywhere in Australia for the treatment of cold symptoms. When camping in the Outback many years ago, one of our party had a bad cold. He decided to sleep on a bed of fresh eucalyptus leaves. He lay back in bliss, and inhaled the beautiful healing fumes. When we awoke in the morning, we beheld our friend burned all over the color of a cooked lobster. The fumes had been far too strong. And he still had his cold.

The Australian's love of billy tea is expressed in this bush ballad:

You may talk of your whisky or talk of your beer,
I've something far better awaiting me here;
It stands on that fire beneath the gum tree,
And you cannot much lick* it—a billy of tea.
So fill up your tumbler as high as you can,
You'll never persuade me it's not the best plan,
To let all the beer and spirits go free
And stick to my darling old billy of tea.
And at night when I camp, if the day has been warm,
I give each of the horses their tucker** of corn,
Then the fire I start and the water I get,
And the corned beef and damper in order I set,
But I don't touch the grub,** though so hungry I be,
I wait till it's ready—the Billy of tea.
— *The Billy of Tea*, Anonymous, about 1840.

*To lick someone or something is to win or do better. It does not mean "to give a beating" as in American usage.

**Grub and tucker mean food.

EGGS 'N ORANGES (outback)

This recipe will not work with emu eggs. You need chook (hen) eggs.

hen eggs
large oranges
salt and pepper

- With a sharp knife, cut out the top of each orange, making an opening big enough for an egg. Scoop out the flesh then insert the egg (leave shell on).
- Prepare a slow fire with plenty of glowing coals. Make small holes in the coals and place the oranges with eggs in the coals. The heat of the fire along with the juice still left in the orange skin, will actually boil your egg. Depending on how hot your fire is, remove egg in orange when cooked (usually about 7 minutes).

This is a great way to get kids to cook eggs. We can't guarantee they'll eat them though.

VARIATIONS: Many quick-cooking foods may be prepared in this way. If you would rather avoid the orange flavor, find a flat rock with a depression (Don't use a wet rock, however—it may explode in the fire and cause injuries). Clean it off, place over a very hot fire, and when hot, break your egg into the natural pan made by the depression in the rock. The egg will cook right before your eyes. Or, cut hole in slice of bread, lay on hot flat rock, break egg into hole. Of course, the standard practice of enclosing the food in wet clay then placing this on the fire is also an effective way to cook. Depending on the clay, though, you might need a hammer to break it open once it has baked.

Attach a green vine or wet string to a safety pin, stick pin through shell of egg, and suspend egg over fire until cooked. Sounds crazy, but it works!

Encase food in banana skins and cook the same as in oranges. Onions may be substituted for oranges. For dessert, core apples, fill with raisins and sugar. If they will fit in orange cases, cook as above, otherwise, coat with clay and cook.

FRIED TIGER SNAKE (outback)

Tiger snakes, one of the most poisonous snakes in the world, are only found in Australia. They are named because of their distinctive yellow and brown stripes. They are not large snakes, as snakes go. The largest we have seen in the bush was about 3 feet. Most are about 2 feet or less, and the thickness of a hot dog. If you are bitten by one, you've probably had it, unless you can get to a hospital for an antidote right away. We strongly recommend that you do not go hunting for one of these nasties, just so you can try out this recipe (though we would be flattered). In case you are foolish enough to track one down, here's how to do it. Actually, tiger snakes are rather timid, and will not attack you unless you happen to stand on them accidentally. If you make a lot of noise walking through long dry grass in summer in a field populated by tiger snakes, you can see the grass swirling, and hear the swishing as the snakes speed away from you.

The way to catch one is to leave food, especially sugar, around your camp. This is no surprise, is it? It's the same way you can catch a bear (or it can catch you!) in North American forests. This is how we had our first (and only) encounter with two tiger snakes, an adult of about 3 feet, and a baby of about 1 foot. They got into our tucker box (food box).

Old hands claim that the best way to kill a tiger snake is to use a pliable long wire that will, with a strong flick of the arm, crack down on the snake's back and break it. One of us tried this, and couldn't get it to work. By far the most effective way is to use a long forked stick to push down on the snake, pinning it to the ground just behind the head. If you are an experienced bushman, you will be wearing strong boots, and with the heel of such a boot, bring it down on the head and crush it. It helps to have a mate do this, or hold the stick down for you.

If you follow these directions you will have yourself a dead snake—at least that's what we think. It is believed that the tiger snake, no matter what you do to it, never dies until sundown.

tiger snake
herbs, preferably chives
salt and pepper
cooking oil

- With a sharp knife, and the snake definitely dead, cut off the head. Draw the knife down the belly from tip to toe (so to speak). Dip the snake into boiling water, then work the point of the knife under the skin at the neck, and loosen the skin all around. Roll back skin, have a mate hold body of snake at neck, peel skin completely off. Remove entrails (not much to remove) or leave and discard after cooking. Cut into sections.

- Heat oil in old bush frying pan until quite hot. Quickly fry snake until golden brown. Serve sprinkled with chopped chives or parsley. If you can find some wild asparagus (sometimes found along the edges of irrigation canals) boil and serve also. Salt and pepper a must. Vegetables are important with this dish. Potatoes (regular, not yams) baked in the fire's coals go nicely with this dish. Do not overcook, or meat will be tough. (It's tough anyway, but then, what can you expect?) Frankly, even though they are poisonous, we'd rather tiger snakes weren't killed. They're part of Australia, after all.

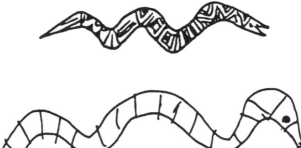

SINGED WITCHETTY GRUBS (outback)

Witchetty grubs (from the aboriginal *witjute,* the name of roots in which the grubs are often found) are various larvae that feed in the wood of eucalyptus trees, most often between the bark and the trunk. They are about 1 to 2 ½ inches long, with a fat creamy body about the width of a man's thumb, and stumpy legs. The Australian Aborigines who live in the outback are said to consider them a delicacy. As with most food taken by the Aborigines in the outback, they eat their witchetty grubs raw. We have never tried them that way. Although there are many "upscale" recipes for witchetty grubs available these days, we prefer the good old outback style.

witchetty grubs
an old piece of metal
salt and pepper to taste
a little cooking oil (optional)
yams

- So you're stuck in the outback without anything except a little salt and pepper! The outback is desolate, often without vegetation, but one is sure to find somewhere a scrap piece of metal left from some failed effort to drive an enormous distance, or maybe from a "Mad Max" movie set.

- Scrub the metal clean, hopefully in a little sand and water from a nearby trickling creek. Prepare a hot, trench fire and place the metal across the top. Immediately place yams in coals beside the fire. After about 1 hour, when the metal is quite hot, drop the witchetty grubs down and rapidly roll across the metal plate. Keep rolling until they are browned all over. Remove from heat, allow to cool. Remove yams from coals. Break open yams and serve each yam with a witchetty grub nestled in the middle.

Allow 2 grubs per person.

One of us has eaten a witchetty grub cooked according to this recipe. It tasted quite delicious, somewhere between roast pork and chicken, and it stayed down, too!

Grub is a word used by Australians to refer to any larvae found in the garden and elsewhere. When we have asked our American friends what a grub is, they invariably reply that it is a "free-loader" and rarely relate the word to insects (real insects that is). Australians have their own word for a freeloader: a bludger.

ABOUT YAMS: Yams are a type of sweet potato cultivated in many parts of Australia and the South Pacific generally. If preferred, ordinary potatoes could be substituted, and cooked in the same manner.

BAKED FRESHWATER EEL (outback)

- Although Australia has a dry climate, there are many small rivers and creeks that run in winter and spring. They are teaming with freshwater eels, as well as other freshwater fish. We include eels in this chapter because they are the easiest to catch (that is to say, they are the *only* darned fish we ever managed to catch). As for fishermen everywhere, a plentiful supply of beer is needed in order to snare these creatures, usually very late at night.

When you hook these eels, you will think you have a shark on the line. They fight to the death, often tearing their bodies off the hook in order to get free.

freshwater eels
old piece of metal
salt and pepper to taste
cooking oil (optional)
yams

- Prepare as for tiger snake (page 264). Prepare fire and hot plate as for Witchetty grubs (page 266) but do not have fire quite as hot. Roll pieces of eel across hot plate. Depending on type of eel and where you caught it, flesh may be quite fatty. Cook until fat has run out. Serve with baked yams.

BUNYIP BUNS (modern outback)

We have saved this recipe for here, abiding by the principle that we have held to since childhood: always keep the best till last. When we were kids, we ate vegetables first, pie crusts and other tasty morsels last.

The bunyip is a mysterious animal (far more mysterious than the Tasmanian Devil) which has been sighted only by the most experienced outback bushmen. One of us can claim to have made at least one sighting, and possibly two, both late at night, during fishing trips with a bunch of mates and a lot of beer. We have spoken to many other experienced outback campers who have also confirmed the existence of this animal.

The bunyip is a diurnal animal, but is so well camouflaged (it not only changes color, but also shape) that it is difficult to distinguish from the grays, browns, and whites of ghost gums (a particular type of eucalyptus tree, made famous by the Aboriginal artist, Albert Namatjira). It is also a cowardly animal, and has been known to hide behind other animals when it observed the barrel of a hunter's gun.

Nothing is known of its reproductive cycle, except the one thing that makes it possible to share this recipe with you. It establishes nesting places made of a strange fibrous substance, rather similar to the truffles dug up in northern Italy. In fact, it is possible to find these bunyip nests using small piglets, properly trained. One must be very lucky to find Bunyip hollows. Although bunyips are sighted mostly where ghost gums grow, one cannot be sure that bunyip nests will be found in the same place. Furthermore, it is claimed by some old timers that bunyips systematically destroy their nests every few days—or at least move them to other places—in order to fool would-be nest farmers.

1 package yeast
1 ¼ cups milk
¼ cup sugar

4 tablespoons butter
2 cups flour
1 teaspoon salt
1 bunyip nest
1 egg
1 cinnamon stick

- Mix yeast with a little warm milk and a little sugar, add rest of milk (warmed) and let stand 10 minutes. Rub butter into flour until it looks like oatmeal, then add sugar and salt.

- Wash and drain bunyip nest well, removing any pieces of fur or feathers that may be attached. Clip off any black pieces—these are old and bitter. A fresh nest will be a rich brown in color and will have a smell similar to that of fresh cut grass. Break in pieces, place in blender, and grind. Add to flour mixture.

- Add yeast mixture and beaten egg. Mix with wooden spoon, and work into soft dough. Knead well, then make balls of dough about half the size of tennis balls and place on greased cookie tray. Cover with damp dish cloth and leave in warm place until dough rises to about double the size. Boil a little sugar with one cinnamon stick in water, and glaze tops of buns. Bake at 425 degrees for about 20 minutes, or until golden brown.

- Serve hot with butter, sprinkle with sugar and cocoa, or powdered hot chocolate.

Glossary

Indigenous Australian Foods

Bugs. Not the insect kind. Term given to primitive looking lobster-like creatures found in the bays and inlets of Australia's northeastern coast. Look something like a lobster tail with eyes and no claws. A somewhat stronger taste than lobster.

Bunya nuts. Australia's own pine nuts, from Australia's native pines. Unless bought commercially, must be boiled for at least 30 minutes.

Bush cucumber. Tastes like a cross between regular cucumber and melon, with maybe a touch of grape.

Bush tomatoes. Said to be a relative of the commercial tomato and potato. Dried and ground, can be substitute for paprika.

Emu. The great Australian flightless bird, resembling the ostrich. Now farmed commercially. The meat is red. The eggs have a strong flavor, and are equivalent to about 10 chicken eggs.

Eucalyptus oil. A well-known oil, now marketed even in the United Sates as a cold remedy. Distilled from Australian gum (eucalyptus) trees. Be sure to use food-grade oil. It's very strong.

Kangaroo and wallaby. This game meat, as with all game meat, is low in fat. Steaks are popular, as are smoked and dried "jerky." You can buy jerky at souvenir shops and airports in Australia.

Kakadu plum. A green olive-size plum very high in vitamin C (some say the highest). May be found manufactured into a jelly.

Kurrajong flour. Made from the ground seeds of kurrajong trees. Makes a tasty spread mixed with macadamia nut oil. As a flour it adds a nutty flavor to breads.

Lemon aspen. This is a small yellow fruit found in Australia's eastern rain forests. Can be used as a citrus substitute.

Lemon myrtle. Tastes a bit like lemon grass. Bake into breads or herb butter. Available commercially at specialty stores in Australia.

Munthari. These are small apple-flavored berries, that grow on creeping plants found among the dunes of southern Australia. They are about the closest thing Australians have to cranberries.

Nardoo. A plant bearing edible seeds from which the Aborigines used to make a paste or dough.

Native limes. There are several species of indigenous citrus fruits, most found in southeast Queensland.

Native mint. There are two edible native mint bushes, with very strong flavor. Recommended for use in sauces such as pesto, or bunya nut butters.

Native pepper. Various plants yield leaves that have a pepper-like quality. Look for Mountain pepper, Dorrigo pepper, or Snow pepper in specialty stores (in Australia, that is).

Quandong. These are a kind of native peach, with a touch of tart apricot. Very popular in Australian country kitchens for jams and jellies. Widely available in Australian supermarkets.

Water chestnut. The Australian species is the same as that found in Asia.

Warrigal greens. A wild spinach that is found around Australian inland waterways. A version of this was used by Captain Cook to fight off scurvy in the 1770s. They are also sometimes called, in the Sydney area, Botany Bay greens.

Wattle. There are about a thousand species of wattle (ranging from trees to shrubs) in Australia. One species produces seeds that are edible, once roasted. Now widely available and promoted in Australian specialty shops and some supermarkets. Use in pasta, ice-cream, breads, and even beverages.

Wild tamarinds. A bright yellow and orange fruit, depending on the species. Good for sauces and dressings.

Witjute grubs. (witchetty grubs) These are the larvae of large moths which lay their eggs in particular wattle bushes. Popular for soups but may even be roasted. They have a nutty, peanut butter flavor, and a pork-like texture.

Yabbies. Small lobsters found in Australia's freshwater streams.

Yams. These are tubers grown in tropical areas. They have a very short shelf life, and thus are not often commercially available. Highly nutritious substitute for potato, and have much more fiber.

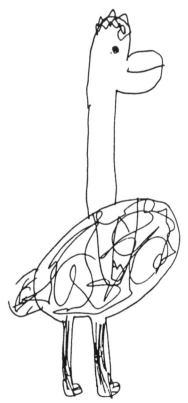

Appendix

Good Food For Sydney 2000

Should our readers be fortunate enough to visit the Olympic Games in Australia in the year 2000, the possibilities to indulge in Australian delights are endless. When on vacation, though, there is little time to cook. Instead, eating out is the way to go, and in Sydney there is much from which to choose. We have listed a small number of restaurants that are highly rated according to the *Sydney Morning Herald Good Food Guide*, which, by the way, you would be well advised to purchase upon arrival. Unless otherwise stated, you can partake of the great Australian tradition and bring your own wine or beer to these restaurants. This is a widely accepted practice. You may be charged a nominal "corking fee" for glasses and serving the wine.

AUSSIE CLASSICS

It used to be that the surest way to find the classic Aussie foods—the meat pie, pasty, or sausages—was to go to any Australian pub and have a "Counter Lunch." In these colorful places, as in England, one buys a glass of beer, chats with one's mates (friends), and orders from a long menu written up on a large board. These days, many of the pubs have expanded their offerings to include dishes from many other ethnic cuisines. But most pubs still offer the classics. The prices are usually much below those of restaurants.

Robin Hood Bistro, 203 Bronte Road, Waverly. Phone: 9386 0674. As the name suggests, this restaurant is not exactly "Australian." Excepting that, as we suggest in the introduction to this book, much of the traditional Aussie dishes are actually English. Here you can try pasties, steak and kidney pie, bangers (sausages), and Irish Stew. And there's plenty of good Aussie wine.

Barbecued Foods

Centennial Park Cafe, corner of Grand and Parkes Drives, Centennial Park. Phone: 9360 3355. Barbecued whole fish is a favorite these days and you will find it here.

Plaza Grill, 36 Blue Street, North Sydney. Phone: 9964 9766. Anything you can barbecue is offered here, but the specialty is steak, aged and otherwise. And don't forget the great Australian favorite: lamb.

Scones and Tea

Vaucluse House Tea Rooms, Wentworth Road, Vaucluse. Phone: 9388 8188. Try exotic as well as traditional teas here, along with excellent fluffy scones with jam and cream. Can't get more Australian than this.

THE AUSSIE MELTING POT

Just about any restaurant that lists itself as "Australian" has a melting pot menu. Try some of these:

Verona Cafe Bar, 17 Oxford street, Paddington. Phone: 9360 3266. One can get quite a range of dishes here from Moroccan lamb with couscous, pizzettas, Peking duck, Thai beef salad, and a whole range of Italian pasta. And for a touch of Australia, try the unusual fig and frangipani tart.

The Red Center, 70 Alexander St., Crows Nest. Phone: 9906 4408. We're talking pizza here. From Tex-Mex toppings, to Thai chicken pizza, not to mention the goat's cheese and olive purée. Good wine. Moderately priced.

The Palace, Corner of Flinders and South Dowling Streets, Darlinghurst. Phone: 9361 5170. Try this for a melting pot soup: roast beet root and ginger soup, with a dash of coconut cream and lime. You can also get pasta, borscht, and duck, then finish with poached strawberries. Moderately priced.

FISH

Fish abound in the waters around Australia's enormous coastline. Here are a couple of great Sydney restaurants that combine fish and a great view of one of the greatest harbors in the world.

Pier, 594 New South Head Road, Rose Bay. Phone: 9327 6561. Take the ferry to Rose Bay, enjoy the view of the harbor on the way. Then dine at the Pier. It may be a bit expensive, but it's worth it. You shouldn't leave Australia without trying one of its most popular fish, barramundi. You can get it here, simply grilled, with olive oil and lime. You might try the crab tart as well. Enjoy the fabulous view.

Rozelle Fishbowl, 580 Darling Street. Phone: 9555 7302. If you can't afford to splurge at the Pier, try this quiet little place hidden away in Sydney's inner suburb of Rozelle. There's a choice of fresh fish of the day, barbecued or deep-fried, and big chunky chips (French fries)—unlike any you'd find in the U.S. This place is simple quality, and moderately priced, too.

OUTBACK COOKING:
"MODERN AUSTRALIAN"

Well, outback no more. "Modern Australian" cuisine has reinvented, or should we say simply invented Australian food using ingredients derived from indigenous Australian flora and fauna. So try these challenging places in Sydney. If you can't visit Australia, try some of the recipes from Chapter 13.

Riberries 'Taste Australia,' 411 Bourke Street, Darlinghurst. Phone: 9361 4929. Here you can try foods with bunya nuts and muntharies, and char-grilled kangaroo. There's emu prosciutto as well. Even the very traditional Pavlova (see page 196) is modernized with wattleseed, sugarbark, and native fruit sauce. Moderately expensive. If you don't know what some of these ingredients are, have a look in our Outback Cooking chapter for a brief explanation.

Edna's Table, Lobby Level, MLC Center, Martin Place, Sydney. Phone: 9231 1400. Now this place offers some really original Aussie dishes that depend on genuine Australian indigenous ingredients. Try, for example, the rich kangaroo broth, Northern Territory (Australia's northeastern most territory) Magpie goose, or maybe grilled rudderfish on native aniseed oil. This is a strange experience—a true taste of Australia. It can be expensive.

WINES

It's hard to know where to start writing about Australian wines. In the past 15 years, the Australian wine industry has exploded, and the Aussies, once geared only to beer as their favorite alcoholic beverage, have become more and more appreciative of the wonderful wines that Australian wineries now produce. (This is not to say, of course, that Aussies have reduced their beer drinking. Not at all! They have simply added on to their drinking pleasure, that of wines of many varieties.) A favorite pastime of many Australians is to drive through the countryside and visit the many wine-tasting wineries. If you have time while in Sydney, the Hunter Valley is the place to go.

The first grapes were planted in the Hunter Valley sometime in the early nineteenth century. After many trials and tribulations, not the least of which was the Aussies' lack of interest in wine, a wine boom arose in the 1970s, and many wineries have flourished since then. Now, the Hunter Valley is considered a producer of wine of international excellence. The wines are described as "big, though soft in character." The area produces wines ranging from dry Hunter semillon to sweet spatlese and sauternes. There are now well over 50 wineries in the lower and upper Hunter Valley. We could describe and list the most famous wineries to visit, but frankly there are too many of them, and we just hate to select any above the others. We strongly recommend that the visitor contact the visitor center at Cessnock where one can get plenty of free advice, brochures, and guides. Cessnock Visitor Center, Turner Park, Aberdare Road, Cessnock, Australia. Write to: P.O. Box 152, Cessnock, 2325, Australia. Phone: 049-904477. Fax: 049-906954. Also available are accommodation guides, guided tours, maps, guidebooks, and much else.

As for the wines, we recommend tasting a few of the following, although we just hate to single any out. Of course, by the year 2000 many new wines will be available, and many older wines will have aged.

Chardonnay is probably the white wine that is most popular among Aussie wine drinkers. But because of the climatic diversity of Australia, the chardonnays themselves vary enormously. There are also many blends of semillon which are also popular. Try, for example, the Banrock Estate Semillon Chardonnay (1996), fruity touch (about $7.00 [Australian] in October, 1996). Peter Lehman Semillon, 1995. "wonderful dry white wine." ($10.00 Australian).

Allendale Chardonnay, 1995. $17.00 (Australiana). Full flavored and crisp.

Red wines are probably the old favorites of Australian wines, having made their mark in the 1960s, even before the wine boom of the 70s. Try Banrock Station Shiraz 1994, $11.00 (Australian). Very full spicy fruity flavor. Seppelts Harpers Range Cabernet Savignon, 1994. About $14.00 (Australian). Rich with berry fruit depth, touch of oak. Tyrrell's Old Winery Cabernet Merlot 1995. $14.00 (Australian). From one of the oldest wine making families of the Hunter Valley district.

A guide for those who are wine aficionados is the Penguin Books *Good Australia Wine Guide* by Mark Shield and Huon Hooke. There are countless hundreds from which to choose, and prices are quoted as up to date as possible.

Mail-order sources are available, it if you are having trouble locating authentic Australian ingredients. You can send away for Vegemite and other products at:

Kangaroo Connection
Australian & New Zealand General Store
1113 West Webster Ave.
Chicago, IL 60614
(773) 248-5499
 http://www.suba.com/%7Ekangaroo/food.html.

Or

The Australian Catalog Company
7412 Wingfoot Drive
Raleigh, N.C. 27615
Phone: 1-800-808-0938, fax: 919-878-0553

One can purchase a wide variety of Australian foods and other items of Australiana from these mail-order stores.

Index

Index